Boulder
Cooks

Boulder Cooks

Recipes and Profiles
from
Boulder County's
Best Kitchens

Janis Judd

Boulder, Colorado
1996

Text by Janis Judd
Copy Editors – Kate Neale Cooper, Jennifer Newens
and Mary Jo Lawrence
Book Design and Composition by Paulette Livers Lambert

ISBN 0-9634607-8-1

3D Press, Inc.
P.O. Box 7402
Boulder, CO 80306-7402

Acknowledgments

I am very lucky to have family and friends who have supported me in everything I have attempted to do throughout my life. Outside of my family and friends, I was most influenced by Julia Child. Some day I hope to see her again, for my star-struck voice failed me the only time I had a chance to meet her. M.F.K. Fisher has also been a source of great inspiration to me for her beautiful writing and her courage in fighting a debilitating illness, Parkinson's Disease.

I thank each and every one of you who has loved me and encouraged me to follow my dreams. Thanks, Mom, for all the junior baking kits, the pasta machine and *Mastering the Art of French Cooking*. Thanks Dad for lobster tail at the French Tavern every Sunday and for eating and praising my first attempts at cooking. *Boulder Cooks* would not have happened but for my daughter Jessica's faith in me. Thanks Jess for getting your mother a publisher! And Niff, what can I say? Besides your wonderful support, you are my expert consultant and advisor.

Some of my favorite times have been spent in the kitchen cooking with friends and family. My children have constantly challenged me to try new things and keep up with the latest trends in cooking. I am indebted to many friends with whom and for whom I have cooked—making Chinese dinners with Sandra and Sharon; preparing gourmet meals with Pat, Marie, Carlyn and Joyce; making sausages at 2 am with Paul; my first buttercream with Gia; Helen's sharing ideas for Tastes and Tales; learning Bugialli's techniques with Pat; making my first wedding cake for Penny and Garland; cooking Cajun specialties with John; sharing recipes with Lynda, Diane, Betty, Emily, Dottie, Donna, Kerry Bella Vista and many others I don't have room to mention. A very special thank you to Rosemary who inspired me, cooked with me and introduced me to Paris. I also want to thank Lyndall who allowed me to cook in her home when I was kitchenless.

To everyone who participated in *Boulder Cooks*, I owe a huge debt of gratitude. Each of you was so encouraging and enthusiastic, you made my job a joy. I was fortunate that Dave Rich of 3D Press was willing to take a chance on an amateur and continues to believe in me. And to Nancy Nelson: we have worked on many a cookbook and newsletter, all of which have been made beautiful by your artwork. I am so pleased that you are a part of this publication which is so close to my heart! Thank you especially for "little Janis." To the most important person in my life, Dick Judd, I cannot begin to express my gratitude. You are my husband, my lover and my best friend; you have always been my #1 fan no matter what I have attempted to do or wanted to pursue. "I love how you love me!"

—Janis

Contents

What makes the city and county of Boulder so unique? It's the quality of life that residents cherish—the great weather, incredible scenery and world-class restaurants. Boulder's best known landmark, the Flatirons, mark its front-range-of-the-Rockies location, 40 miles northwest of Denver. With its unique location and climate, you can ski powder in the morning at nearby Eldora, be back in Boulder for lunch and then go for a bike ride or climb world-class routes in Eldorado Canyon in 60-degree sunshine in the afternoon.

Boulder is home to the Colorado Music Festival, the Bolder Boulder 10K national championship running race, Boulder School of Massage, the Naropa Institute and the University of Colorado. Within the city limits are 25,000 acres of open space, 56 parks and 150 miles of biking and hiking trails. It is estimated that there are more bikes (93,000) than people (86,000). You can listen to Bach or Big Head Todd, "crawl" the Pearl Street Mall or see a Shakespearean drama. You can drive one-half hour to downtown Denver to see the Denver Art Museum or the Broncos, or 1½ hours to some of the best ski resorts in the world. There's a little something for everyone.

Boulder County, 741 square miles of incredible beauty and abundant Colorado sunshine, has 230,000 inhabitants living in a diverse group of cities and towns. Longmont, in the fertile St. Vrain River valley, was named for Major Stephen H. Long (Long's Peak); Lafayette is the location of the richest coal vein ever found in the county; Louisville, which also supported the coal industry, is known for its Main Street Italian restaurants; and Nederland, situated at 8,000-plus feet, is a former gold mining boomtown that is now a favorite hangout of mountain sports enthusiasts. However, perhaps the most eclectic community is the county seat, the City of

Boulder, known affectionately (and often with tongue-in-cheek) as "the People's Republic of Boulder."

To truly understand Boulder, one must first learn a little about its beginnings and its evolution into the 1990s. Settled in 1858, Boulder was a muddy, ramshackle mining camp. In 1860, a large gold deposit was discovered 12 miles west and 3,000 feet up in the town of Gold Hill. People and dollars flocked to the area. Boulder's greatest economic boost occurred in 1876, when the University of Colorado was founded (an entity that now brings an estimated $700 million into the community annually).

Boulder was incorporated in 1918 and immediately began to shed its "shoot-'em-up cow town" image. Boosted by the University, Boulder's economy has always been cutting edge. During the 1950s and '60s, scientific and environmental research companies, including Ball Aerospace, IBM and the National Center for Atmospheric Research began moving to Boulder. The advent of the computer age propelled Boulder into the high-tech community it is today. As the millennium nears, Boulder's rare combination of city and mountains is attracting lifestyle product companies such as Schwinn and Pearl Izumi.

Residents of Boulder are a mix of university people, high-tech employees, entrepreneurs, professional athletes, students, families and seniors—all of whom just enjoy the lifestyle. The typical Boulderite is a walking, running, cycling contradiction: laid-back, environmentally conscious and uniquely accepting of alternative life styles, yet obsessive about fitness of mind, body and spirit and wild about the outdoors. Boulder has a personality all its own. When Boulderites visiting other places are asked where they are from, they say, "Boulder." Not "Boulder, Colorado"—just, "Boulder."

Notes

Boulder Dining Introduction

When asked what dining out was like in Boulder 30 or 40 years ago, most long-time residents start with the story of The Lamp Post. Until the 1970s, The Lamp Post and The Harvest House Hotel were the only places in Boulder where one could have a drink before dinner or enjoy a glass of wine during the meal. The two establishments were in a small circle of land exempt from local liquor restrictions. The rest of the city was dry and remained so until voters approved liquor licensing in 1969.

The repeal of liquor restrictions, the arrival of high-tech companies with sophisticated employees and a growing population looking for diverse dining experiences made Boulder very attractive to new restaurants of every culinary stripe. Many of the restaurants and chefs chosen for this cookbook have been in business for many years—a pretty good indication of quality. *Boulder Cooks* introduces some of best new chefs in town, as well as a collection of "foodies"—talented cooks who are not professional chefs or restaurant owners, but who are involved in and are passionate about food and cooking. Every recipe has been tested to ensure satisfaction. So . . .

Enjoy and *Bon Appétit*!
Janis B. Judd

Notes

Before Beginning

Before beginning to prepare a recipe from this book, please review the following information. It will help you achieve the very best results. You may also want to refer back to it occasionally for certain recipes.

In general, be sure to carefully read all the way through a recipe before preparing it for the first time. Have all of the ingredients, as well as utensils and other needed equipment, ready before you begin. It will save time and confusion if you do as much advance preparation as possible.

A Word About Ingredients:
It goes without saying that the better the quality of the ingredients, the better the results will be. In this cookbook we do not specify, for example, "extra virgin olive oil, first cold press" each time olive oil is called for, or "freshly ground black pepper" each time pepper is used.

Ingredients:
Balsamic vinegar – true balsamic vinegar, which has been aged over time in several different wooden barrels, is very difficult to find here. Native Italian balsamic is thicker and sweeter than what is imported to the United States. A pinch of brown sugar helps make the balsamic vinegar available to us more like the genuine article.

Butter – when butter is called for, we mean salted butter. Unsalted butter is specified if required. If you wish to substitute margarine, be aware that the results will be different.

Eggs – we used Grade A, large eggs for all recipes.

Flour – use all-purpose flour unless otherwise specified.

Herbs – dried herbs were used in this book unless fresh herbs were specified in the recipe. As a general rule, you can substitute one teaspoon of dried herbs for one tablespoon of fresh, chopped herbs and vice versa.

Mixed greens – many markets now offer mixed greens so that you do not have to purchase a head of radicchio, a head of

Bibb lettuce, a bunch of arugula, etc. Examine the greens closely to make sure they are very fresh. Some stores let the greens sit out until they are sold and you may end up with a wilted salad. If premixed greens are not available at your market, the following varieties are a good mix: Bibb, Boston and romaine lettuce, endive, radicchio, arugula, oak-leaf, escarole and frisée.

Olive oil – the best olive oils are extra virgin, first cold press. All olive oils are cold pressed; the key word is "first." *Fine* virgin olive oil is less flavorful, while *pure* olive oil is a blend. *Extra mild* or *light* olive oil is often used in baking, especially in Italian recipes. In general, the deeper the oil's color, the more intense the flavor. A good rule of thumb is to use a lesser-quality olive oil if you are going to cook something in it. Use a better oil when you are not going to heat it (e.g. if you are making salad dressing).

Onions – unless specified, use yellow and white onions interchangeably.

Parmesan cheese – the only authentic Parmesan is Parmigiano Reggiano. There is a distinctive difference between Reggiano and other Parmesans. Reggiano is available in specialty cheese stores, Italian markets and some groceries.

Pepper – pepper means black pepper, preferably freshly ground.

Vanilla – always use pure vanilla extract, not imitation. The difference is significant.

Vegetable oil – in all recipes calling for vegetable oil, we have used canola oil.

Terms:
Chopping – the terms used in this book for chopping are, from smallest to largest, mince, finely chop, chop, coarsely chop, and cube or dice. Mince means to cut into tiny pieces. Finely chop means to cut into very small pieces. Chop means to cut into ¼" to ½" pieces. Coarsely chop means to

cut into pieces which are over ½" thick. To cube or dice is to cut into little blocks (the size is indicated in the recipe).

Zest – the colored part of the skin of citrus fruit. The zest is removed with a vegetable peeler and minced, or removed with a citrus zester. Before you remove the zest, wash the fruit with soap, rinse it thoroughly and dry it. Use only the colored part of the skin, not the bitter white pith underneath.

Equipment:
Knives – always keep your knives sharp. If you do not have a steel or a sharpening stone, buy one and learn to use it properly. Always keep your knives clean (wash them by hand, the dish washer dulls them). They are one of the biggest sources of food cross-contamination. Cut food on wood or composition cutting boards. Cutting on metal, glass, granite or marble will ruin your knives. Good knives are one of the best investments you can make in the kitchen; they are about the most basic pieces of equipment you have and good knives make cooking easier and more enjoyable.

Pots and pans – in this book, all frying or sauté pans are called skillets. The size of skillet to use depends on the amount of food being cooked in it. The same goes for saucepans. If a very large pan is required, we call it a stockpot. A baking dish is an oven-proof metal or glass container or casserole with sides.

Methods:
This cookbook assumes you have a knowledge of common kitchen practices and good hygiene, such as washing your hands, rinsing chicken and other foods before using them and refrigerating perishables. If a recipe calls for a change in common procedures, it is specified in the text.

Blanching – plunge food into boiling water for a brief period (10 to 15 seconds) and then place it in a bowl of ice water. This process heightens color and flavor. It also helps loosen the skin to make peeling easier for certain nuts, fruits, and vegetables.

Clarifying butter – clarified butter is used when higher temperatures are called for; it will not burn as easily as regular butter, but it imparts a similar flavor. To make one-half cup of clarified butter, heat one stick of unsalted butter (or more, if needed) to the boiling point in a medium saucepan. Heat on low until the milk solids separate and the mixture looks clear, like vegetable oil. Skim off the top foam. Pour off and reserve the clear liquid, discarding the milk solids that collect in the bottom of the pan.

Hot chiles – the utmost care should be taken when handling hot chiles. Chiles exude an oil that stays on anything it touches. Wash everything that has come in contact with cut chiles: the knife, the cutting board and, most especially, your hands. If you are especially sensitive, use rubber gloves. [Contact lens wearers should be especially careful. The publisher of this book, who is a great chile lover, scrubs his hands with salt and then with soap before touching his eyes or lenses.] As a general rule, always remove the white, spongy ribs and the seeds from the chiles before you chop or mince them. These parts contain the greatest concentration of capsaicin, the compound that makes chiles hot. An easy way to remove the seeds and membranes from chiles is to cut off the stem end and run a grapefruit knife or vegetable peeler around the inside of the chile, getting rid of the seeds and membranes without having to touch the inside of the chile.

Peeling peaches – plunge peaches into boiling water for about 10 or 15 seconds, depending on the ripeness of the peach. Remove immediately and allow to cool. The skin should come off easily.

Peeling tomatoes – plunge tomatoes into boiling water for about five seconds and remove immediately. The skin should slip off easily.

Risotto – it is not difficult to make risotto, but there are no shortcuts. The basic technique is the same for every risotto recipe: cook the rice in hot oil until well coated and slightly translucent; then while stirring constantly, add small amounts of liquid (usually broth). As soon as one addition of liquid is absorbed, add the next. The risotto is done when it is tender but firm (al dente) and bound with a creamy sauce. Always serve risotto immediately; it will tighten and lose its creamy consistency as it cools. Arborio rice is essential for risotto. Superfino Arborio is the best. It is available in many groceries and specialty food markets. If you absolutely cannot find Arborio rice, use a domestic short-grain rice; never use converted rice.

Roasting and peeling peppers – there are many ways to roast and peel peppers. One method is to line a baking sheet with aluminum foil (this saves having to wash the pan after) and preheat the broiler. Put the peppers in one layer on the baking sheet and broil for three to four minutes, then turn them. Continue broiling and turning the peppers until all sides are blistered and slightly charred but not black. Immediately seal the peppers in a brown paper bag to steam them. After 10 or 15 minutes, remove the peppers. The peppers should now peel easily. Remove the skin and seeds, and prepare the peppers according to the recipe. Other methods of peeling a pepper include holding the pepper over the flame of a gas stove or placing it directly on the grill.

Steaming – a method of cooking where food is placed on a rack, above boiling liquid. The steam produced by the liquid cooks the food. Steaming retains more of the food's vitamins and minerals than other cooking methods and, in some cases, helps hold the shape of the food.

Sweating – to sweat means to cook in a covered pan over low heat in a small amount of fat until the food softens and releases moisture. Sweating onions releases the sugars in the onion and imparts a sublime, slightly sweet flavor to the food (carmelizing).

Water bath – also called a *"bain marie,"* a water bath is a cooking method whereby food is placed in a container which is then placed in a larger container of hot water coming about half-way up the sides of the smaller container. This method is used for delicate dishes such as custards or flans. It is also a great way to keep food warm, especially sauces that will spearate, such as hollandaise.

Roasing garlic – roasting makes garlic much ore mellow. To roast: Cut about 1/2" off the top of whole bulbs of garlic (opposite the root end). Drizzle with olive oil and season with a little salt and pepper. Place in a baking dish and cover with heavy duty aluminum foil, or use a clay garlic baker. Roast in a preheated 400 degree oven until tender (approximately 45 minutes). You can also roast whole unpeeled cloves. They will take less time to become tender.

About Altitude:

The recipes in this book have been tested at an altitude of approximately 5,200 feet. If you live at a significantly higher or lower altitude, you may want to adjust the amounts of certain ingredients and the cooking or baking times.

For every 1,000 foot increase in altitude from sea level, water boils at a temperature two degrees lower. In Boulder water boils at 203° compared to 212° at sea level. At higher altitudes allow a little longer time when cooking in water. At lower altitudes watch that food doesn't over-cook. A rule of thumb is to boil foods four percent longer per each 1,000 feet gained and four percent shorter per each 1,000 feet lost. Baking or roasting also takes less time at low altitude; check for doneness five to 10 minutes earlier than the time specified in the recipe.

When baking at high altitude, use slightly less sugar, shortening or butter, baking powder and yeast, and more egg white, cream of tartar, liquid, and flour. Do the opposite at low altitude. Since water evaporates faster at high altitude, baked goods may need more liquid. Increase the liquid in the dough or batter by teaspoons until you get the proper texture. The baking powder in cookie recipes should be increased and the sugar slightly decreased when prepared at a higher altitude. At low altitude, the opposite is true in each case (except do not increase the sugar). There are differing opinions as to the exact amount of this and that to add or subtract when you are changing a recipe which has been tested at an altitude different from yours. Understanding the effects of higher altitudes and experimenting will help you more than anything.

To the memory of
Geoff Sherin
1963-1997

One of Lyle Davis's favorite things to do is show off the fields of flowers and vegetables at Pastures of Plenty, his home and one of his businesses. "These are old-fashioned frying peppers," he says, pointing to rows of green leaves with small red peppers. "And those are Romanian peppers, they're kind of thin-skinned and yellow with a rosy blush." As you walk with him, you get the feeling that this is where he truly feels at home. We sit in Davis's backyard, at a rustic table under a large apple tree that shades us from the sun. It's reminiscent of the French or Italian countryside. His family, complete with dog and cat, joins us as he relates his story.

Davis grew up in the Hudson River Valley north of New York City. "My love of food and gardening came from my family and our place in upstate New York. We had a beautiful 150-year-old farmhouse with four acres of gardens." Both of his parents loved to garden. His mother was also a remarkable cook, says Davis. "I really learned to appreciate food and to love gardening from her. She also loved gathering friends and family around a table; there were always lots of people in our home."

Davis's mother grew up in Paris, but her father was Italian – an influence that was present in his childhood. In the 1960s, Davis's family was eating arugula and dandelion greens with baby lettuces from their garden. Fresh pesto was common at their table. "This was way before this stuff was known and popular in the U.S.," he says.

When Davis was 17, he went to school in Mexico and caught the travel bug. For several years thereafter, whenever he had enough money, he would travel: to Africa, to Europe and so on. When he was 25, Davis came to Colorado to work with his father, who had received a grant from Rutgers University to experiment with hydroponic greenhouses in hostile environments. The location chosen for the experiment was Elbert, Colorado, at 6,700-feet.

Alfalfa's Market/ Pastures of Plenty

Lyle Davis, Co-founder/ General Manager, Alfalfa's Market Owner, Pastures of Plenty

4039 Ogallala Road, Longmont
440-5220

The money Davis saved while working with his father provided him with funds to invest in the Pearl Street Market with partner Haas Hassan and Mark Retzloff in 1979. That business evolved into Alfalfa's Market in 1981. In the beginning, the store was run by Davis, Hassan, Louie (a boyhood friend of Davis's) and two cashiers. Louie's wife did the bookkeeping. "We all had to know how to do every job in the store in those days," says Davis.

Today, Davis is somehow able to juggle raising a family, building a major addition to his house (actually combining two old farmhouses), running the gardens at Pastures of Plenty and working his job at Alfalfa's. His recipes reflect his appreciation for the best and freshest ingredients available, and for gathering friends and family around the table.

Pasta Santa Clara

Serves: Four to Six

"The village of Santa Clara lies just down the road from Assisi," relates Davis. "It's named for Umbria's 'other' famous saint, Saint Clara. Outside the bustle of Assisi's tourism, this sleepy working town boasts one of Italy's great local *trattorie*. Foreigners have to wait to enjoy their meal until lunch has been served to the local folks, who seem to have reservations ad infinitum, but the wait is worthwhile. My wife, Sylvia, and I had this pasta dish at one of Santa Clara's *trattorie* during a brief visit to Italy."

1. In a large skillet, heat the oil and then add the pancetta and onion. When the pancetta is starting to get crisp and brown, and the onion is turning translucent, add the garlic and cook for another few minutes. Add the white wine and red pepper flakes and bring the mixture to a boil. Reduce the mixture by half, then remove it from the heat.

2. While the pancetta mixture is cooking, cook the pasta according to the package directions. When the pasta is approximately three minutes from being done, place the arugula in a small colander or sieve and plunge into the boiling pasta water for 30 seconds, then remove and drain.

3. Heat the pancetta mixture over medium-high heat. Add the arugula and cook, stirring, for two minutes. Add the cream and cook over medium heat. When the pasta is done, drain it and add it to the mixture in the skillet. Reduce the heat and cook, stirring constantly, until the pasta is well incorporated; about two minutes. Serve immediately.

*TIPS
—Pancetta is an Italian meat similar to bacon, used to flavor all kinds of dishes. It will keep in the freezer for up to 6 months. You can find it at specialty markets. You can substitute bacon for the pancetta, but the flavor will be different because pancetta is not smoked.

½ cup olive oil
1 (1½") piece pancetta*
1 yellow onion, chopped
4 garlic cloves, minced
¾ cup dry white wine
1 tsp. red pepper flakes
1 lb. uncooked macaroni or
      other elbow-style pasta
2 large bunches arugula
      (preferably large-leafed,
      mature arugula)
1 cup heavy cream

Grilled Eggplant with Shallots and Tomatoes

Serves: Six to Eight

Davis says, "When eggplants are overtaking our back fields at Pastures of Plenty, usually in late August, we love to make this dish for our harvest crew suppers."

2 medium eggplants
¾ cup olive oil, approximately
4 shallots, minced
juice of 2 lemons
1 bunch Italian parsley, finely
    chopped
2-3 tomatoes, chopped into
    ¼" pieces
salt and pepper

1. Slice the eggplant into ½"-thick rounds. You can leave the skin on if the eggplant is fresh. Generously brush the eggplant with olive oil and grill on both sides. Do not allow the eggplant to char. Remove the rounds from the heat when they are soft and pliable.*

2. In a medium skillet, heat two tablespoons of olive oil. Cook the shallots in the oil over medium heat until they are soft. Add the lemon juice, parsley (reserving a little to garnish) and tomatoes. Add salt and pepper to taste. Cook for four minutes, stirring occasionally. Remove from the heat.

3. Place the eggplant slices on a platter creating a concentric circle. Parallel the eggplant circle with a 2" band of the shallot mixture. Sprinkle with the reserved parsley. Serve warm or cold.

TIPS
—An outdoor grill is best for cooking the eggplant, but the grilling can also be done under the broiler.

Braised Chicken with Sweet Peppers

Serves: Four

This is an old Alfalfa's favorite from Davis's days managing the market's commissary. He recommends serving it with risotto or pasta. You can prepare it through step 3 in advance and finish steps 4 and 5 later.

1. Combine the thyme, salt, pepper and flour in a plastic bag. Add the chicken pieces to the bag and toss until pieces are well and evenly coated.

2. Heat the olive oil over medium heat in a heavy skillet (cast iron works best). Add the chicken pieces and brown them on all sides. Remove the chicken to a platter and cover with foil.

3. Add the onion to the same skillet. Cook the onion until it is almost translucent, stirring to loosen the brown bits left over from the chicken. Stir in the garlic. Cook until it is barely starting to brown, then add the wine. Reduce the wine slightly over medium heat.

4. Return the chicken to the skillet with the onion mixture and add the tomatoes and oregano. Cover the pan and simmer for 35 minutes.

5. Add the roasted peppers. Cover and simmer for an additional 10 to 15 minutes. Taste and correct the seasoning as necessary. Serve on a large, warm platter. Sprinkle with chopped parsley.

1 Tbl. dried thyme
1-2 tsp. salt, or to taste
1 tsp. pepper, or to taste
3 cups flour
1 whole chicken fryer, cut into
    8 pieces
⅔ cup olive oil
1 medium yellow onion,
    chopped
4 garlic cloves, thinly sliced
1 cup dry white wine
1 (28 oz.) can whole, peeled
    tomatoes
1 Tbl. dried oregano
3 large yellow bell peppers,
    roasted, peeled, seeded
    and cut into ½" strips (see
    "roasting and peeling peppers
    in Before Beginning)
coarsely chopped Italian
    parsley to garnish

Andrea's German Cuisine

Andrea Liermann, Chef/Owner

216 East Main Street, Lyons
823-5000

A scenic drive north from Boulder along the foothills of the front range brings you to Andrea's Restaurant in Lyons. Chances are Andrea herself will welcome and guide you to a table in one of the cozy dining rooms reminiscent of Bavaria.

Andrea grew up in Germany on an estate located at the tip of a finger of land surrounded on three sides by East Germany. "I was born in a beautiful, beautiful place, far away from any big city," Andrea explains. "In spite of the changes taking place in Germany at the end of World War II, I still had a wonderful childhood." Some of her first memories are of picking blueberries and gooseberries for her family's hotel and restaurant, so it is not surprising that Andrea ended up in the restaurant business.

Andrea came to Boulder in 1965 with her former husband, an exchange student at the University of Colorado. It was only natural for her to work in a restaurant, and she was employed by several around Boulder. After a brief return to Germany, Andrea came back to Colorado for good. She and her son, Mark, moved into a house near Lyons and she started working at the Black Bear Inn. "One day, a friend told me that she wanted to sell the old Mobil gas station that she had made into a fast food restaurant. The dream of opening my own restaurant was always in the back of my mind." Though the asking price was more than Andrea could afford, she and her friend were able to come to terms and Andrea's German Cuisine became a reality.

The menu at Andrea's includes traditional German dishes such as sauerbraten and red cabbage as well as lighter fare, such as pastas and fish. Andrea was kind enough to share some authentic recipes from her family. These are the real thing!

Andrea's Sauerbraten

Serves: Six

This recipe takes three or four days to prepare, so plan accordingly. Andrea serves the sauerbraten with dumplings, pasta or potato cakes, and red cabbage.

1. Combine the vinegar, water, onion, bay leaves, carrot, pepper and salt in a saucepan and bring to a boil. Cover and simmer over low heat for 30 minutes. Cool.

2. Place the roast in an oven-proof baking dish just large enough to hold it, and the vegetables and liquid from step 1. Pour the vinegar and vegetable mixture over the beef. Cover and place in the refrigerator for three or four days, turning the beef at least once a day.

3. Preheat the oven to 350°. Before roasting the meat, drain and discard the marinating liquid, reserving the vegetables. Dry the meat with paper towels. Coat a skillet with the oil and brown the meat on all sides over high heat. Return the meat to the baking dish or place it in a roasting pan, along with the marinated vegetables, tomatoes, broth and wine (fresh vegetables such as onions, carrots and turnips may be added, if desired). Top the roast with the bacon, cover and place it in the oven for 60 to 90 minutes, until the beef is very tender.

4. Remove the meat from the casserole and strain the roasting juices. Pour ½ cup of the strained juices back into the casserole. Over medium heat, whisk in the flour. When thoroughly blended, add the remaining roasting

⅓ cup cider vinegar
½ cup water
1 onion, peeled and stuck with
    3 whole cloves
2 bay leaves
1 large carrot, peeled and
    halved
1 Tbl. black peppercorns
1 Tbl. salt
2 lbs. lean beef for roast
    (e.g. eye of round)
1-2 Tbl. canola oil
7 tomatoes, peeled, seeded and
    chopped (or one 28 oz. can
    diced tomatoes)
2 cups beef broth
1 cup dry red wine
cut-up onions, carrots and/or
    turnips (optional)
5 slices bacon
¼ cup flour
1 Tbl. tomato paste (optional)
salt and pepper

juices and bring the mixture to a boil, stirring constantly until the mixture thickens. If needed, add more flour to get a gravy consistency.* Add tomato paste, salt and pepper to taste. To serve, slice the meat and top it with plenty of gravy.

*TIPS

—If you need to add more flour, mix it with a little tomato paste first, then whisk it into the sauce, otherwise the gravy may end up lumpy.

Thuringian Potato Dumplings

Serves: Six as a side dish

"In my longtime cooking experience, these dumplings are the most difficult to master," says Andrea, "but well worth the effort because they are delicious. Serve them with a good roast topped with lots of tasty sauce and a great salad."

8 slices stale bread
4 Tbl. butter, melted
2 lbs. russet potatoes, peeled
1 tsp. + 1 tsp. salt

1. Preheat the oven to 275°. Trim the crusts from the bread slices and brush each slice on both sides with the melted butter. Cut the bread into ½" cubes and place them on a baking sheet in a single layer. Bake for approximately 30 minutes, stirring and turning occasionally. When done, the bread should be dried and lightly browned. Set aside to cool.

2. Coarsely grate two-thirds of the potatoes (1⅓ lbs.) into a bowl of cold water. Let the potatoes sit for 10 minutes. Drain the potatoes, reserving the starch that collects

in the bottom of the bowl. Place the grated potatoes in a large towel and squeeze out as much moisture as possible. Place the potatoes in a large bowl and sprinkle lightly with one teaspoon salt.

3. Place the remaining one-third of the potatoes ⅔ lb. in a saucepan and cover with water by about 2". Add one teaspoon of salt. Bring the potatoes to a boil and cook until they are very tender. Without draining the water, mash the potatoes. Return the potatoes to a boil and then pour the mashed potatoes over the dry, grated potatoes. Add the reserved starch and beat until the mixture forms a smooth, sticky dough.

4. To form the dumplings, wrap potato dough around a few of the bread cubes to form a ball (be sure the bread cubes are completely encased inside). The ball should be 2" to 2½" in diameter. It helps to wet your hands when forming the dumplings. Cook the dumplings in gently simmering, salted water for 10 to 15 minutes. Serve immediately.

Apfelstrudel

Serves: Six to Eight

Strudel is a pastry made with many layers of paper-thin dough. Andrea has included her family recipe for making the dough. If you do not want to go to the trouble of making the dough from scratch, you can substitute commercial phyllo pastry sheets.*

1½ cup flour
large pinch of salt
1 egg, beaten
⅓ cup warm water
1 stick of butter, plus more if
    needed, melted

1 cup fresh breadcrumbs,
    browned in butter
8 cups peeled, cored and
    coarsely chopped Granny
    Smith apples
1 cup golden raisins
1 tsp. cinnamon
½ cup sugar

1. On a flat surface, sift the flour into a mound. Sprinkle the salt over the mound and make a well in the middle. Beat the egg and water together and pour into the well. Stir the mixture with a fork, gradually incorporating the flour until a soft dough is formed (you may need to add a little more water). Knead the dough until it becomes soft and elastic. Place the dough in a warm bowl and cover it with a cloth. Let the dough stand in a warm place for 30 minutes.

2. Cover a large flat area, such as a table top, with a cloth or sheet and sprinkle it lightly with flour. Roll out the dough until it is as large and thin as possible. Brush the dough with melted butter to keep it from drying. Make a fist and pull and stretch the dough with your palms down. Brush the dough with butter several times during this process.

3. Preheat the oven to 325°. Evenly spread the breadcrumbs, apples and raisins over the dough. Mix the cinnamon and sugar together and sprinkle all but two tablespoons of it over the filling. Using the cloth to help you, roll the dough into a large cylinder-shape. Brush the dough with butter and place it on a lightly buttered (or parchment paper-lined*) baking sheet. Bake for approximately 45 minutes, or until the pastry is golden brown and the apples are tender. Sprinkle the strudel with the remaining cinnamon-sugar and serve warm with *shlag.**

*TIPS

—If using commercial phyllo dough, spread one sheet on a flat surface and brush it with melted butter. Top with another sheet and brush with butter. Repeat until you have seven or eight layers, then continue with step 3.
—Parchment paper is available in most cookery stores and some groceries.
—Shlag is whipping cream lightly sweetened and beaten until thickened but not stiff.

Bistro St. Tropez

To satisfy a craving for authentic soupe à l'oignon, try the Bistro St. Tropez in Niwot, a warm, friendly restaurant reminiscent of its namesake, the seaside resort on the French Riviera. Bistro St. Tropez is owned by Hervé Lequien, a native of Amiens, France, a town 60 miles north of Paris. Lequien says of his business, "My intention was to create a bistro, which in France is a neighborhood restaurant and wine bar. It is less formal than a traditional French restaurant where you go for a five-course dinner. It's a place that offers more provincial food, where people can afford to eat two or three times a week."

Lequien attended the hotel school in Strasbourg, France – in the Alsace region near the German border. After graduating, he worked on a cruise ship for five years, until 1975 when emigrated to the United States. He started in Atlanta, then moved to Dallas in 1978. He remained in Texas for 17 years during the growth years, opening a new restaurant about every six months for the company he worked for. Becoming frustrated with big city life, Lequien started looking for a location where he could open his own restaurant. He had been skiing in Colorado, and had spent time in Boulder as well.

"Boulder itself was saturated with restaurants," says Lequien. "Plus the rents were too expensive." He liked the area around Niwot and found a restaurant that was for sale. "The location is super; it's just five or 10 minutes from Longmont, Louisville and Gunbarrel, and 15 minutes from downtown Boulder." An interior designer friend transformed the dining room of the former Mexican restaurant, giving it new windows and furniture, and painting the walls a traditional French mustard color.

On the menu at Bistro St. Tropez are les hors d'oeuvres, such as scampi provençales and escargots bourguignonne. Entrées include such specialties as steak au poivre, chicken marsala or cioppino. Chef Gary Seamon prepares several pasta dishes and makes a true minute steak. Typically splendid French desserts abound.

Hervé Lequien,
Chef/Owner

7960 Niwot Road,
Niwot
652-0747

Moules Marinière (Mussels with Shallots, Herbs and White Wine Sauce)

Serves: Four as an appetizer

Lequien has found that the most readily available mussels are green-lipped mussels from New Zealand.*

1 lb. green-lipped mussels, well
    cleaned
2-3 Tbl. olive oil
4 shallots, minced
2 garlic cloves, minced
1 cup dry white wine
1 tsp salt
1 cup water
1 Tbl. minced fresh basil
1 Tbl. minced fresh oregano
1 Tbl. minced fresh thyme
4 Tbl. butter, cut into 4 equal
    pieces
minced fresh parsley to garnish
lemon wedges to garnish
crusty French or
    sourdough bread

1. Place the mussels in a large stockpot or saucepan. Add the olive oil, shallots, garlic, wine, salt, water, basil, oregano, and thyme. Bring to a boil, then cover the pan. Steam until the mussels open.

2. In each of four warmed soup or pasta bowls, place one tablespoon of the butter and approximately ½ cup of the cooking broth. Divide the mussels among the bowls. Sprinkle with parsley and garnish with lemon. Serve with bread.

Variations:
Moules Poulettes: Add two to three tablespoons heavy cream to the sauce in each of the bowls.
Moules Dijonnaise: Add two to three tablespoons heavy cream whisked with one teaspoon of Dijon mustard to the sauce in each of the bowls.

*TIPS
—Choose mussels with tightly closed shells or ones that shut when tapped. Discard any mussels with broken shells. To clean, use a stiff brush to remove all sand, grit and mud from the outer shell. Pull the dark, shaggy beard away from the shell.

Chicken Niçoise

Serves: Four

The chicken needs to be marinated for a few hours, so plan accordingly. This dish is delicious and simple to prepare for company because you can make it in advance to the point when it goes in the sauce for the final cooking. Lequien suggests serving by itself with a fresh vegetable or slice it on the bias and serve over pasta.

1. Place the chicken breast halves in a bowl with ½ cup of the olive oil, rosemary, thyme, salt, pepper and the bay leaf. Toss and marinate in the refrigerator for at least two hours.

2. While the chicken is marinating, make the sauce. Place the one tablespoon of olive oil in a medium skillet. Over medium heat, add the shallots and cook until soft. Add the tomatoes and garlic. Cook for five minutes, stirring often. Add the olives and wine, and simmer for 10 minutes.

3. Grill the chicken over high heat for just long enough to show grill marks on both sides. Place the chicken in the skillet with tomato mixture (you can stop at this point and reheat just before serving).

4. Just before serving, heat the chicken and sauce together over medium heat. When the chicken is cooked through, about five minutes, sprinkle it with the basil and cook, covered, for another three minutes over low heat.

*TIPS
—Kalamata olives are Greek or Mediterranean olives that have a delicious, but strong, flavor. They can be found in jars in many groceries and fresh in specialty stores and delis.

2 skinless chicken breasts, halved
½ cup + 1 Tbl. olive oil
1 tsp. dried rosemary
1 tsp. dried thyme
¼ tsp. salt
¼ tsp. pepper
1 bay leaf
¼ cup minced shallots
2 large tomatoes, peeled, seeded and chopped (see Before Beginning)
2 garlic cloves, minced
½ cup seeded and coarsely chopped Kalamata olives*
1 cup dry white wine
½ cup chopped, fresh basil leaves

13

Bistro St. Tropez chef Gary Seamon was kind enough to share one of his favorite recipes. It comes with a story that explains the reason for the name of this recipe, Truite du Jardin de Jacques (*Trout From Jacques' Backyard*).

When Seamon was attending cooking school, Jacques De Chanteloupe was teaching the charcuterie class. De Chanteloupe asked Seamon to split and then halve four pigs feet. Seamon misunderstood and cut the pigs feet into 16 pieces. De Chanteloupe flew into a rage when he saw what Seamon had done and shouted, "They are ruined. You have ruined the lesson for the entire class!" Seamon was mortified and worried throughout the term that he was going to fail the course.

On the final day of the term, the class was making pâté en croûte. De Chanteloupe had prepared an edible clock face in the center of the pate. "I remarked that I thought of a way to make the hands move every time the pate was sliced," explains Seamon. "Jacques responded, 'This is not possible.' But when I explained my idea to him, he was impressed enough to let me try. It worked and I ended up with a 98 in the class."

Seamon and De Chanteloupe became close friends, sharing their mutual love of fishing and making frequent trips to the Adirondacks to fish. The first time they went, Seamon said that the fish De Chanteloupe had caught were too small and that he should throw them back. "Jacques replied, 'I never mind, I know how to fix them.' It's the smaller trout that he would use in this recipe because the pin bones dissolve.

"I treasure the memories of the lunches we would have along the river, sitting on the tailgate eating garlic sausage and pâtés and drinking his homemade cider. But, most of all, I treasure the friendship that we shared as two fishing chefs."

Truite du Jardin de Jacques (Trout from Jacques' Backyard)

Serves   Four as a first course or Two as an entrée.

Seamon prefers to grill the trout over very hot coals. He recommends putting the grill closer to the coals than usual.

1. Place the trout on the grill. When they begin to scorch, turn them over and quickly scorch the other side. Remove to a tray.

2. Move the grill up a notch or two and place a medium, cast iron skillet over the coals. Melt the butter in the pan. Add the shallots and cook them until translucent, but do not brown them. Add the cream and season with salt and white pepper to taste.

3. Place the trout in the skillet and gently simmer for three minutes. Turn the trout and cover the pan. Simmer for another three or four minutes, then remove the lid. Reduce the cream (with trout still in the pan) until the cream is thick enough to coat the trout without running off it. Serve immediately.

*TIPS
—Some variations are to stir in a dash of amaretto and top the trout with toasted almonds; or add a little pesto and diced sun-dried tomatoes to the sauce.

4 small trout, cleaned
2 Tbl. butter
¼ cup minced shallots
2 cups heavy cream
salt and white pepper

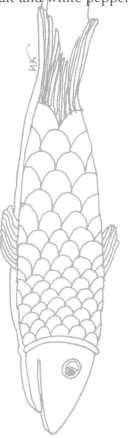

Tiramisù

Serves:　　　Six to Eight

3 Tbl. espresso
1 Tbl. + 1 tsp. sugar
1 Tbl. coffee liqueur
24 ladyfingers*
8 oz. mascarpone cheese
½ cup heavy whipping cream
1 tsp. vanilla
cocoa powder

1. Combine the espresso, one tablespoon of sugar and the liqueur. Stir until the sugar dissolves. Dip 12 of the ladyfingers in half of the espresso mixture. In a 10" baking dish, place the ladyfingers in two rows of six each.

2. Whip the Mascarpone with the whipping cream until smooth. Add the 1 tsp. of sugar and the vanilla. Blend well. Spread half of the mascarpone mixture over the ladyfingers. Sprinkle with a little cocoa powder.

3. Dip the remaining 12 ladyfingers in the espresso and layer atop the first ladyfinger-mascarpone layer. Top the second ladyfinger layer with the remaining Mascarpone. Cover and refrigerate for at least two hours or overnight.

4. Finish each serving with a dusting of cocoa powder.

*TIPS
—Italian or "savoiardi" ladyfingers are preferred, but homemade ladyfingers also work well. Italian lady fingers are available at specialty markets. The ladyfingers available in the grocery are also okay.

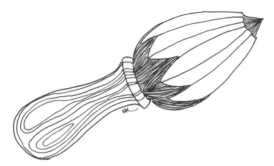

Bookend Cafe

The first thing you notice upon walking into the Bookend Cafe are the wonderful smells; the aroma of freshly brewed coffee blended with hints of pastries and desserts just out of the oven. Former general manager "Lou" Boches said, "One of the smartest things we did was to move the baking in-house."

Early in 1992, when Phil Shull was considering opening a coffee bar next to the popular Boulder Book Store, he consulted Boches—a wise choice. Boches was well qualified to get the Bookend started. She worked in the pantry of the former Pelican Pete's. When it closed, she followed the chef (now her husband Joe) to Pete's Prime. She gained still more experience when she and her husband started the catering business, Ala Carte. Boches added another paragraph to her resumé at Alfalfa's, spending four years as the Boulder store's kitchen manager.

The Bookend is attractively arranged. The walls are exposed, original brick. Displayed near the cash register are brightly colored T-shirts sporting the Bookend Cafe logo, as envisioned by several local artists. Tables are arranged so that you can find a quiet spot for a private conversation or sit in a busy section perfect for seeing and being seen. Since Boulderites love to sit outside any time the sun is shining and the temperature is above freezing, the outdoor tables are open nearly every day.

Although Boches has left the Bookend, her distinctive touch remains. The coffee menu is extensive. The glass counter to the right of the register shows a tempting variety of baked goods. Freshly baked pies, such as the Raspberry Sour Cream that Boches shares with us, are available to go.

Pastries and lattes are not the only culinary delights to be found at the Bookend. It was Boches's idea to serve other food as well. A large chalkboard against the back wall lists salads, homemade soups, sandwiches and delicious hot entrées, all of which are available to eat

Linda "Lou" Boches, Former manager

1115 Pearl Street, Boulder
440-6699

at the cafe or to take out. Many of the offerings are arranged in a large display counter; attractive, colorful and obviously fresh, they are hard to resist.

French Potato Salad

Serves: Eight

This salad can be served hot, cold or at room temperature.

8 cups quartered small red
        potatoes (3 to 3½ lbs.)
extra virgin olive oil
½ cup Champagne Vinaigrette
        (recipe follows)
¼ cup minced parsley
2 Tbl. minced fresh thyme
½ cup mayonnaise
2 Tbl. minced garlic
¾ tsp. salt
¾ tsp. pepper

1. Preheat the oven to 425°. Brush the potatoes lightly with olive oil. Place the potatoes on a baking sheet in a single layer and roast until golden brown, turning after about 20 minutes. Set aside to cool slightly.

2. Mix the remaining ingredients and toss them with the warm potatoes. Allow the salad to stand for at least 30 minutes. Serve at room temperature or chill in the refrigerator. If serving the salad warm, toss the potatoes with the vinaigrette immediately after taking the potatoes from the oven.

Champagne Vinaigrette

Makes: 2½ cups

½ cup extra virgin olive oil
1 cup canola oil
½ cup champagne vinegar
2 Tbl. Dijon mustard
¼ cup finely chopped green onion
1 Tbl. chopped parsley
½ tsp. salt
¼ tsp. pepper

Whisk together all of the ingredients. Use on any vegetable salad.

18

Tuna Vegetable Loaf

Serves: Eight

This dish can be prepared in advance and reheated.

1. Preheat the oven to 350°. In a medium skillet, cook the onion, celery and carrots in a little olive oil. When the vegetables are soft, add the garlic and cook for a few minutes longer. Do not allow the garlic to brown. Transfer the mixture to a large mixing bowl.

2. Add the remaining ingredients and mix lightly until well-blended. Press the mixture into a loaf pan that has been lightly sprayed with oil. Bake for 45 to 60 minutes, or until the center of the loaf springs back when you push on it (or the internal temperature reaches 180°). Cut the loaf into eight slices and garnish with sprigs of dill.

¾ cup minced yellow onion
½ cup minced celery
¾ cup minced carrot
olive oil
1 Tbl. minced garlic
2½ cups canned solid white tuna (apx. 4 cans), drained and slightly broken up
1¼ cups milk
¼ cup chopped parsley
6 large eggs, beaten
2 Tbl. fresh lemon juice
¾ cup grated Cheddar cheese
2 Tbl. chopped dill (or 2 tsp. dried)
½ tsp. dried thyme
½-1 tsp. salt
½ tsp. pepper

Raspberry Sour Cream Pie

2 large eggs
1¼ cups sour cream
1 cup + ¼ cup sugar
¾ cup + 2 Tbl. flour
½ tsp. vanilla powder* (or 1
    tsp. vanilla extract)
¼ tsp. salt
3 cups raspberries, fresh or
    unsweetened frozen
    (thawed)
1 unbaked 10" pie shell
1 stick of butter
½ cup pecans

Makes: One 10" pie

1. Preheat the oven to 350°. In a mixing bowl, beat the eggs. Add the sour cream, one cup of the sugar, the two tablespoons of flour, vanilla and salt. Mix until smooth. Place the raspberries in the unbaked pie shell and top with the sour cream mixture. Smooth the sour cream mixture evenly over the berries. Bake for 30 to 40 minutes.

2. While the pie is baking, make the streusel topping. Process ¾ cup of the flour, the butter and ¼ cup of the sugar in a food processor until the mixture resembles cornmeal. Stir in the pecans by hand.

3. Remove the pie from the oven and top it with the streusel. Return the pie to the oven for 15 to 20 minutes, until the pie is set. Place the pie on a rack to cool. The pie will set more as it cools. If not serving within a few hours, refrigerate the pie after it cools.

TIPS
—Vanilla powder may be difficult to find, but it's worth the extra effort.

"*B*oulder has everything," says Jim Smailer, chef for 16 years at the The Boulder Cork. "There is nowhere else I want to live." Smailer is an avid biker and he feels the combination of the weather and the multitude of bike paths cannot be beaten. Originally from Philadelphia, Smailer moved to Colorado because his wife was a graduate student in the music department of the University of Colorado. Smailer's lifelong dream was to pursue a career with the National Park Service. However, the Park Service was not hiring when he was looking, and Smailer had to consider other employment.

He turned to cooking. Smailer came from a family of cooks who encouraged his interest in food. His grandfather was his greatest influence. "He was a naturalist and he opened my eyes to lots of bits and pieces of nature that I apply in my cooking," Smailer explains. The inspiration Smailer gained from his grandfather is evident at The Cork in the fresh and natural ingredients used to prepare each dish.

Wife Kate teaches piano full time but is also a great cook and an exceptional pastry chef, says Smailer. The Smailers often cook together, both for friends and for many events benefiting Boulder County. Smailer enjoys preparing and eating fish. One example is his Grilled Salmon with Chanterelles on Garlic and Wild Mushroom Mashed Potatoes, the recipe for which he shares with us.

The Boulder Cork

Jim Smailer, Chef

3295 30th Street,
Boulder
443-9505

Artichokes, Fava Beans and Pecorino on Arugula

Serves:　　　Six

This delicious salad or first course is a favorite of Smailer's.

2 large artichokes
juice of ½ lemon
3 lbs. fresh fava beans*
½ lb. arugula*, washed and
　　dried, with tough stems
　　removed
¼ lb. Pecorino Romano*
　　cheese, sliced paper thin
1 Tbl. fresh lemon juice
½ cup extra virgin olive oil
1 Tbl. red wine vinegar
salt and pepper

1. Cut the stems off of the artichokes. Place the artichokes in a large saucepan with 1" of water and the juice of ½ lemon. Cover and steam the artichokes for approximately 30 minutes, or until the stem ends feel tender when stuck with a fork. Watch that the water does not boil away; add more if needed. Remove the artichokes from pan and let cool. Once cool, remove the leaves and the chokes—the fuzzy center—(a grapefruit spoon works well), leaving just the hearts. Cut each of the hearts into six wedge-shaped pieces.

2. Remove the fava beans from the pods. Blanch the beans to help remove the tough skin (see Before Beginning).

3. Arrange the arugula on six salad plates and top each with two artichoke wedges, some fava beans and the Romano cheese.

4. Whisk together the one tablespoon of lemon juice, olive oil and vinegar. Season with salt and pepper. Drizzle the dressing over the salad.

TIPS
—Fresh fava beans are available in late spring and fall, but can be difficult to find, even in season. If you can find favas, look for ones without beans bulging in the pods, which show aging. If you cannot find fava beans,

you can substitute fresh baby lima beans.
—Arugula is a type of lettuce with flavors of pepper and mustard. If you substitute another type of lettuce, you will get an entirely different taste.
—Pecorino Romano cheese can be found in specialty markets and some groceries. If you substitute a domestic, or lesser-quality Romano the dish will not be as good.

Asian Beef Rollups

Serves: Six as an appetizer

These are not on the menu at The Cork, but they are available for private parties. Note that the meat needs to marinate overnight.

1. Combine the pineapple juice, ½ cup of the soy sauce, wine and one tablespoon of the ginger. Add the steak to this mixture, cover and marinate overnight.

2. Grill the steak to medium-rare. Set aside to cool and then refrigerate until cold (this makes slicing easier). Slice the steak very thinly.

3. Place a dollop of cream cheese in the center of each slice of beef. Add several sprouts and bell pepper strips. Roll the beef strips around the filling. Wrap each rollup with one or two slices of pickled ginger. Secure with a toothpick and place on a platter.

4. Combine the vinegar, mirin, sesame oil, the two teaspoons of soy sauce and the ground ginger. When you are ready to serve, sprinkle the rollups with the vinegar mixture and top with sesame seeds.

1½ cups pineapple juice
½ cup + 2 tsp. soy sauce
½ cup dry red wine
1 Tbl. grated ginger
1½ lbs. top sirloin
8 oz. cream cheese
1 package daikon sprouts*
1 red bell pepper, cut into thin
   strips
8 oz. pickled ginger*
2 Tbl. rice wine vinegar
2 Tbl. mirin*
1 tsp. toasted sesame oil
½ tsp. ground ginger
black sesame seeds, toasted
white sesame seeds, toasted

*TIPS
—Daikon is also called Oriental radish. They can be found in Asian markets and in many groceries. Daikon sprouts are usually available throughout the year. If unavailable, substitute radish sprouts or some other slightly spicy sprout.
—Pickled ginger and toasted sesame oil can be found in Asian markets or in the Asian section of the grocery.
—Mirin is a slightly sweet, Japanese cooking wine. You can substitute one tablespoon of a medium-sweet sherry for two tablespoons of mirin.

Grilled Salmon with Sautéed Chanterelles

Serves: Six

Smailer serves the salmon on Roasted Garlic and Wild Mushroom Mashed Potatoes (recipe follows).

2 Tbl. extra virgin olive oil
1 Tbl. coarse Dijon mustard
juice of 1 lemon
salt and pepper
6 (6-7 oz.) salmon fillets
1 lb. fresh chanterelle mushrooms*, whole if small, or sliced if larger
2 Tbl. unsalted butter

1. Whisk the olive oil, mustard and lemon juice together. Season with salt and pepper. Set aside for basting the salmon.

2. Cook the salmon on a hot grill for six to eight minutes, turning once and basting often. Remove the salmon from the grill and keep warm until the chanterelles are cooked.

3. Sauté the chanterelles in the butter for six to eight minutes, until just tender. Season with salt and pepper.

4. To serve, place mashed potatoes on each of six warm plates. Divide the salmon into six portions and place atop the potatoes. Spoon sautéed chanterelles on top.

*TIPS

—Chanterelles are a yellowish-colored mushroom with a frilly, trumpet-shaped head. They are available in late summer and early fall. Do not put them in a plastic bag or they will become soft and slimy. Instead, refrigerate them in a box or paper bag covered with damp paper towels. Wipe off any dirt with damp paper towels; do not rinse or soak them in water because they will absorb the water and lose their flavor.

Roasted Garlic and Wild Mushroom Mashed Potatoes

Serves: Six as a side dish

Smailer says, "The key to great mashed potatoes is to work fast and not to over whip."

1. Preheat the oven to 425°. Place the garlic in a pie pan, cut side up. Drizzle the bulbs with olive oil and lightly season with salt and pepper. Cover with heavy-duty aluminum foil and roast until tender; about 45 minutes. Separate the cloves and squeeze the tender pulp from the skins. Place in a food processor and purée completely.

2. While the garlic is roasting, boil or steam the potatoes until tender.* Peel the potatoes as soon as they are cool enough to handle and place them in a large mixing bowl. Mash the garlic purée, the olive oil and four tablespoons of the butter with the potatoes. Gradually add the milk and beat until it is incorporated and the potatoes are smooth (a few lumps are okay).

4 whole bulbs of garlic, top 1/2" cut off
extra virgin olive oil
salt and pepper
4 large russet potatoes, unpeeled
2 Tbl. extra virgin olive oil
6 Tbl. unsalted butter, at room temperature
2 cups milk
½ lb. mixed wild mushrooms

3. Cook the mushrooms in the remaining two tablespoons of butter, until tender. Coarsely chop the mushrooms and season them with salt and pepper.

4. Stir the mushrooms into the potatoes. Add salt and pepper to taste. Keep warm until serving.

*TIPS
— The purpose of cooking the potatoes with their skins on is to preserve as much nutritional value as possible. Any treatment that exposes more of the potato to water, e.g., peeling, results in higher losses of important nutrients such as vitamin C and the B vitamins. As a general rule, place the potatoes in already-boiling water, as the longer the exposure, the more vitamin C is lost.

How did a homemaker and mother of two become the second woman in the United States and just the third in the world to earn the title Master Sommelier!? "Purely by accident," says Sally Mohr. After high school, Mohr began working for Storage Technology. She never imagined that she would become one of the most knowledgeable oenophiles (connoisseurs of wine) in the nation, much less achieve the status of Master Sommelier.

Mohr worked for Storage Tech for five years, then married in 1980 and had two children. Finding that life in a big corporation was unrewarding, Mohr resigned. She wanted something to do but was at a loss for a career that would be challenging.

Mohr and her husband had become interested in wine and her husband suggested she ask the owner of their local wine shop for a part-time job. Neither suspected where this would lead.

Working in the shop sparked Mohr's interest and she decided to take some classes on wine. During this time, she met Wayne Belding, who was also working at the wine store. In 1986 Mohr and Belding purchased the Boulder Wine Merchant. Belding, who earned his own title of Master Sommelier in 1990, encouraged Mohr to pursue her interest as well, and in 1993 she signed up for the first level of the sommelier course.

To reach the coveted designation of Master Sommelier, one must pass three levels of exams. Sally passed the written exam for level one, doing well enough to try for level two. Level two consisted of three parts: a written exam, a taste test and a hands-on service exam in a restaurant-like situation. The tasting section requires students to taste and describe each of six wines for "color, aroma and flavor — taking it as far as you can go," explains Mohr. Passing with flying colors, she began studying for the final stage.

Boulder Wine Merchant

Sally Mohr,
Co-owner,
Master Sommelier

2690 Broadway,
Boulder
443-6761

Working with Belding at the Wine Merchant was a great help in reaching her goal. "We would practice, tasting different wines all the time." Mohr smiles, "Believe it or not, I really got sick of it. I would ask for a day off with no tasting." Level three consisted of a tasting and a service exam, but has an oral rather than a written section. Mohr passed the tasting portion, but not the service or oral parts. "They asked things like, 'What is the most common variety of grape used to make wine in Russia?'" The next chance to take the exam was held in England and Mohr flew off to London to try again. This time she aced the test and became the second woman in the United States to achieve the title.

Through her work at the Boulder Wine Merchant, Mohr is trying to "take the snobbery out of wine; to bring good, affordable wine to everyone." She insists, "Every person should be able to enjoy wine with every single meal. It's no longer just for the upper income community."

Mixed-Grain Pancakes

Makes: 12 to 15 pancakes, depending on size.

½ cup whole-wheat flour
1 cup buttermilk
½ cup rolled oats
¼ cup yellow cornmeal
2 Tbl. canola oil
2 tsp. baking powder
½ cup plain low-fat yogurt or
     ricotta cheese
1 egg
¼ cup wheat germ
½ tsp. baking soda

1. In a bowl, mix all of the ingredients, stirring until no lumps remain. Let stand for 15 minutes.

2. Place a skillet or griddle over moderately-high heat and brush (or spray) it with a small amount of oil. When the griddle is hot, place spoonfuls of batter on it (the size is up to the chef). When bubbles start to form on top of the batter, flip the pancake with a metal spatula and cook until the other side has turned golden brown. Serve immediately with fresh fruit or your favorite syrup.

Broiled Sea Bass with Shiitake Mushrooms

Serves: Four

Mohr serves this dish with rice and a salad.
She recommends a Pinot Noir to accompany the fish,
rather than a white wine.

1. Fry the diced bacon in a medium-sized skillet until
crisp. Drain the bacon on paper towels and set aside,
reserving all but one tablespoon of the drippings.

2. Remove the stems from the mushrooms and chop
them into ¼" dice. Place them in the skillet with the
reserved bacon drippings and cook over moderate heat
until soft. Add the garlic and parsley and cook, stirring,
for one minute. Add the water and oyster sauce, and
cook for one minute longer. Return the diced bacon to
the skillet and sprinkle the mixture with a pinch of
nutmeg. Keep the mixture warm on the stove.

3. Preheat the broiler. Season the sea bass with a little
salt and pepper. Place one slice of bacon on each side of
the fish and broil the fish, turning once, until it's cooked
through. Discard the bacon slices.

4. Place the fish in the skillet with the mushroom mixture and spoon the mushrooms over it. To serve, divide
the fish into four portions and top with the mushroom
mixture.

5 slices bacon; 3 slices diced,
     2 slices left whole
4 oz. shiitake mushrooms
1 garlic clove, minced
2 Tbl. minced Italian parsley
4 Tbl. hot water
1½ Tbl. oyster sauce*
pinch of nutmeg
1 lb. fresh sea bass
salt and pepper

*TIPS
—Oyster sauce can be found in Asian markets or the
Asian section of the grocery.

Sally's Favorite Cookies

1½ cups flour
2 tsp. baking powder
1 tsp. salt
1 stick butter, at room
    temperature
⅔ cup sugar
⅔ cup packed dark brown
    sugar
1½ tsp. vanilla
1 ripe banana
2 large eggs
½ cup rolled oats
1½ cups wheat germ
12 oz. semisweet chocolate
    chips

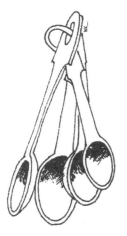

Makes: 24 large cookies

1. Preheat the oven to 350°. Coat two or three cookie sheets with nonstick cooking spray or a thin layer of butter or shortening.

2. Sift together the flour, baking powder and salt. Set aside.

3. Cream the butter with an electric mixer. Beat in the sugar, brown sugar, vanilla and banana. Add the eggs and beat well.

4. With the mixer on low speed, beat the flour mixture into the butter mixture until just blended. Add the oats and wheat germ. Mix until blended. Stir in the chocolate by hand.

5. Roll the dough into balls using ¼ cup of dough per cookie. Place the cookies on the prepared cookie sheets. Allow plenty of room for the dough to spread while baking (about 4½"). Use a wet fork to flatten the cookies to a thickness of about ½". Bake two cookie sheets at a time (unless you have a convection oven) for 18 to 20 minutes, until the cookies are light brown and the tops spring back when pressed.

6. Cool the cookies for five minutes on the cookie sheets, then transfer them to racks. When cool, place the cookies in an air-tight container.

Celestial Seasonings Cookbook: Cooking with Tea

Jennifer Siegel, co-author

Celestial Seasonings Tea Company,
4600 Sleepytime Drive, Boulder
581-1311

*M*ost Boulderites have heard Mo Siegel's story: he started gathering herbs in the Rocky Mountains for tea and ended up with the incredibly successful tea company, Celestial Seasonings. His wife, Jennifer, has taken the subject of tea one step further by writing *Celestial Seasonings Cookbook: Cooking with Tea* (1996, Park Lane Press, New York), a cookbook of recipes with one thing in common: each contains Celestial Seasonings teas.

Jennifer Siegel comes from a New York family that loves to cook and eat. She still craves the ethnic foods she enjoyed when she was growing up. Many Boulder residents know Siegel's cooking from the Italian dinners she has prepared for local benefits featuring her grandmother's tomato sauce recipe.

Jennifer met Mo while working as a professional actress. She had been asked to represent a health food company as their spokesperson. To learn about the company, she decided to attend a health food show in Las Vegas at which the company was exhibiting. Mo Siegel was representing Celestial Seasonings at the same show. Describing their first meeting, Siegel smiles, "For me it was love at first sight. For him it took a little longer." She moved to Boulder when she married Mo in 1987 and became an instant mother to Mo's three children. She and Mo have since had two children together.

Jennifer is as enthusiastic about food as any professional chef fresh out of a culinary school. She is also a very talented and inventive cook. She says the idea of using tea to season all kinds of dishes happened accidentally. "I was trying to find something to make steamed carrots a little more interesting. Just for the fun of it, I threw in some Mandarin Orange Spice tea bags." Amazed at the great results, she took a closer look at what went into the tea. "I realized that the ingredients in Mo's teas read like a shopping list for a gourmet restaurant."

She experimented with other dishes and teas, and her book (co-authored with Mo) began to take shape.

Siegel's cookbook is a feast for the eyes and the taste buds. It has color photos of many dishes, as well as family photos and the critically acclaimed illustrations from the Celestial Seasoning tea boxes.

Siegel's recipes are delightfully tasty and simple. There are recipes for every course, all containing Celestial Seasonings tea blends.

Brie With Strawberry Kiwi Cranberry Sauce

Serves: Four

"When some unexpected quests popped in, I ransacked my fridge for something to serve and found this leftover sauce from a traditional turkey dinner," Siegel says. "I love the combination of fruit and cheese.

1 cup water
3 Celestial Seasonings Strawberry Kiwi tea bags
1 cup sugar
3 cups whole cranberries, fresh or frozen
1 (1 lb.) wheel of Brie, at room temperature
½ cup chopped walnuts, toasted (optional)

1. Bring the water to a boil in a heavy saucepan. Add the tea bags and simmer for five minutes. Remove the tea bags. Add the sugar and cranberries to the tea and simmer for one hour, stirring every 10 minutes.

2. If serving right away, pour the hot cranberry mixture over the Brie and garnish with the walnuts. If the cranberry mixture is cold, pour it over the Brie, garnish with walnuts and place the cheese in a 300° oven, until it begins to show signs of melting. Serve the Brie with plain crackers or slices of French bread.

TIPS
—Use plain crackers that have no distinctive flavor of their own, such as onion or sesame seed.

Mandarin Orange Spice Meatballs

Serves: Ten as an appetizer

1. Heat the wine in a saucepan until hot, but not boiling. Place the tea bags in a bowl, pour the wine over them and steep for 10 minutes. Set the wine mixture aside and discard the tea bags.

2. In a large bowl, blend the beef, pork, onion, garlic and a large pinch of salt and pepper. Add ¾ cup of the wine mixture and mix well. Form into small meatballs (about 1" in diameter). In a large skillet, heat the oil. Brown the meatballs in batches over medium heat, being careful not to crowd them in the skillet, and adding more oil if needed. Drain the meatballs on paper towels, then place them on a warm platter.

3. Pour out the grease left in the skillet. In a bowl, mix the cornstarch with two tablespoons of the wine mixture and stir until blended. Add the cornstarch mixture and the remaining wine to the skillet. Add the marmalade and cook over medium heat, stirring often, until the mixture has thickened. Return the meatballs to the skillet and simmer for 15 minutes. Taste for seasoning and add salt and pepper as needed.

4. Serve the meatballs with the cooking juices on a platter or in a chafing dish, garnished with strips of orange rind.

*TIPS
—Preparing in advance: The meatballs can be frozen, but the wine-tea mixture will have to be redone when making the sauce. Keep the sauce and the prepared meatballs separate until about 25 minutes before serving, then combine and finish cooking.

1½ cups dry white wine
5 Celestial Seasonings
     Mandarin Orange Spice
     tea bags
1 lb. ground beef
1 lb. ground pork
¼ red onion, diced
1 Tbl. crushed garlic (about
     4 cloves)
salt and pepper
2 Tbl. olive oil
1 Tbl. cornstarch
1 cup orange marmalade
thin strips of orange peel to garnish

Harvest Spice Tea Cake

Serves: Six to Eight

"I like serving this cake straight from the oven with a steaming pot of Harvest Spice tea. The warm, deep golden color of the whipped cream makes this the ultimate breakfast or teatime treat," notes Siegel.

½ cup water
2 Celestial Seasonings
　　Harvest Spice tea bags
3 eggs
¾ cup sugar
1 tsp. vanilla
1¼ cups flour
1½ tsp. baking powder
½ tsp. salt
freshly grated nutmeg
Harvest Spice Whipped Cream
　　(recipe follows)

1. Butter an 8"x8"x2" baking dish. Preheat the oven to 350°. Bring the water to a boil in the saucepan, add the tea bags and simmer for three to five minutes. Set aside.

2. Beat the eggs and sugar together. Add the vanilla and blend well. Mix the flour, baking powder and salt, then add it to the egg mixture. Add the tea, squeezing the liquid out of the tea bags and discard the bags. Add the tea liquid to the batter. Blend thoroughly.

3. Pour the batter into the buttered baking dish and bake for 25 minutes. Sprinkle the top of the cake with freshly grated nutmeg. Serve the cake warm with butter and Harvest Spice Whipped Cream.

Harvest Spice Whipped Cream

1 cup whipping cream, chilled
2 Celestial Seasonings
　　Harvest Spice tea bags
2 Tbl. sugar
freshly grated nutmeg

In a small saucepan, simmer the cream and tea bags together for 10 minutes. Remove the tea bags, squeezing out the excess cream into the pan. Place the cream mixture in a large bowl and add the sugar. Whip until fluffy. Serve with a sprinkle of nutmeg.

The T-Wa Inn on South Federal Boulevard in Denver has won the best Vietnamese restaurant award for six years running in the annual "Best of Denver" issue of the Denver arts weekly, *Westword*. Well, guess what! The "T" in T-Wa stands for Thuy, as in Boulder's Chez Thuy.

Thuy left Vietnam for the United States in 1970. She first located in Washington State, but she had family in Colorado and moved to Denver in 1973. The first T-Wa Inn was actually in Aurora, near Stapleton Airport (D.I.A.'s predecessor). It later moved to south Federal Boulevard in Denver. Thuy's second restaurant, the T-Wa Terrace, opened in 1989 near the Denver Tech Center. Thuy ran that restaurant until 1993. Chez Thuy opened its doors in Boulder in the summer of 1993.

Thuy runs a tight ship. It often appears that she has an extra set of eyes and ears. When you speak to her, you have her full attention, but you sense that she sees and hears everything going on in both dining rooms and the kitchen while you are talking. Thuy's daughter describes her mother as a true gourmet because she makes up most of the recipes herself. "She just throws things together and then says, 'Okay, that works,' and she's right, it does."

Chez Thuy is the kind of place where you want to bring along friends so you can sample more dishes. Though the menu is extensive, everything comes out hot and delicious. There is regular soup, and soup combinations, which are heartier concoctions, great for cold days. Standouts among many appetizer choices are crystal rolls wrapped in rice paper and served with peanut sauce, Vietnamese egg rolls and, the house speciality, deep-fried soft-shell crab. The menu features salads that make a great lunch on their own or serve as a wonderful addition to a multi-course dinner. Entrées include hot pots, seafood, noodle combinations, lamb, beef, pork,

Chez Thuy Vietnamese Cuisine

Thuy Le, Chef/Owner

2655 28th Street, Boulder
442-1700

poultry and vegetarian dishes, as well as five different kinds of fried rice.

Thuy would not give up any of the restaurant's secret recipes, but once you try the ones she has shared, a fish in tomato sauce and her beef salad, you will find yourself craving them again and again.

Ca Sot Ca (Fish in Tomato Sauce)

Serves: Four

Thuy says, "This is a light dish with so much flavor—you will love it. It takes very little time to make."

1 cup vegetable oil
1 (1 lb.) halibut steak or 2 medium butterfish
1 Tbl. butter
1 garlic clove, minced
1 medium yellow onion, chopped
2 green onions, chopped
5 large tomatoes, peeled and cut into 8 wedges (see Before Beginning)
3 Tbl. soy sauce
½ tsp. red or black pepper
2 Tbl. sugar

1. Heat the oil in a skillet over medium heat. When the oil is very hot, add the fish and fry it until it's crispy and done to your liking. Drain the fish on paper towels. Place the fish on a heated platter and cover it loosely with foil.

2. In another skillet, melt the butter over medium heat. Add the yellow onion garlic and sauté until the garlic just begins to brown. Add the green onions, tomatoes, soy sauce, pepper and sugar. Bring the mixture to a boil and simmer for one minute. Pour the sauce over the fish and serve immediately.

Goi Bo (Beef Salad)

Serves: Four

This is a delicious combination of flavors. After the beef and vegetables are cut and the rest of the ingredients measured, the dish can be prepared in about 15 minutes.

1. Cut the beef, onion, carrot and jicama into thin, 3"-long strips. Heat the oil in a large skillet over medium heat. Add the garlic and stir for one minute. Add the meat, vegetables, sugar, salt and red pepper flakes. Stir until the meat is cooked medium-rare to medium and the vegetables are crisp and not overcooked. Squeeze the limes onto the beef mixture while it is still hot.

2. Place the salad greens on a platter. Top with the beef mixture and sprinkle with cilantro and peanuts just before serving.

*TIPS
—Jícama is a large, root vegetable with brown skin and white, crunchy flesh. It can be found in most groceries.

1 lb. lean round tip beef
1 medium yellow onion
1 large carrot, peeled
3 medium jícama, peeled*
2 Tbl. vegetable oil
1 garlic clove, minced
1 Tbl. sugar
1 tsp. salt
1 tsp. red pepper flakes, or to taste
3 limes
2 cups mixed salad greens
1 bunch cilantro, minced (basil may be substituted)
1 Tbl. ground peanuts

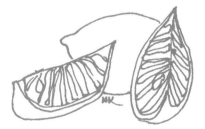

Cooking School of the Rockies

Joan Brett, Director

637-H South Broadway,
Table Mesa
Shopping Center,
Boulder
494-7988

*A*fter 15 years of practicing family law, Joan Brett wasn't having fun anymore. She was burned out and, in 1990, decided to take a seven-month sabbatical. The first part of her time off was spent in a week-long cooking class at the prestigious Peter Kump's New York Cooking School. Joan says, "I was staying with my sister-in-law and after the second day of classes I told her that I was going to open a cooking school. She said, 'Right, and I'm Mickey Mouse.'" But Brett knew that this was what she wanted to pursue.

She met with Peter Kump to discuss the ins and outs of opening a school and returned to his school for a management course. "He was a very kind and generous man. He talked to me about how to get started and how to make it work." Returning to Boulder, she juggled her law practice with the opening of her school. Though Brett took half of Kump's professional courses and studied in France, she doesn't consider herself a professional chef, and says she's most qualified to teach home cooks.

In the beginning, Brett taught classes out of her home, but soon was so successful that she needed a larger location. She found a space at Table Mesa Shopping Center. Brett explains, "It was all brick. There was no storefront, just a concrete shell." She hired an architect who understood kitchens and together they designed the school. The current space is so large that it continues to work in spite of the steady growth of the school — except perhaps for Brett's office which could use a few more square feet these days.

Cooking School of the Rockies (CSR) offers demonstrations and hands-on classes for anyone interested in cooking, as well as basic techniques for more serious cooks and training for professionals. Cookbooks and cooking-related items are sold in the small retail area near the school's entrance. Brett has invited many well-known food authors and chefs to teach at CSR, including Deborah Madison author of *Greens*, Hugh Carpenter of *Hot Wok* and *Fusion Foods* and Stephen Raichlen of the award-winning *Miami Spice* and *High Flavor Low-Fat Vegetarian Cooking.*

Curried Butternut Squash Soup

Serves: Eight to Ten

This soup can be served hot or cold. You may substitute nearly any vegetable for the squash, including carrots or broccoli. "It's simple and delicious," says Brett, "but depends heavily on fresh vegetables, high-quality curry powder and good, clear chicken stock."

1. Melt the butter in a large, heavy saucepan over medium-low heat. Add the shallots, garlic and curry powder. Cook for three to five minutes, stirring often.

2. Add the squash and combine well with the onion mixture. Cover and cook over low heat stirring occasionally, until the onion is tender, 12 to 15 minutes.

3. Add the stock. Cover and simmer for 20 to 30 minutes, until the squash is tender. Cool slightly, then transfer to a blender or food processor in batches and purée. Season with salt and pepper. If serving cold, season the soup after it has chilled in the refrigerator.

4. To serve, ladle the soup into warm or cold soup bowls. Top with a dollop of yogurt and sprinkle with mint.

4 Tbl. unsalted butter
4 large shallots, minced
2 garlic cloves, minced
1 Tbl. high-quality curry powder
2½ lbs. butternut squash, diced peeled and seeded
4 cups chicken stock, or more (or vegetable stock for a vegetarian soup)
salt and pepper
nonfat plain yogurt to garnish
minced fresh mint to garnish

Fillets De Saumon Au Sauce De Tomates (Broiled Salmon Fillets with Tomato Coulis)

Serves: Four to Six

This is a simple but delicious way to prepare salmon that takes very little time. You will need a sharp knife to cut the salmon.

2 lbs. salmon fillets, with skin intact
olive oil
1 cup crème fraîche*
¼ cup Moutarde de Meaux*
2 Tbl. olive oil
2 garlic cloves, minced
2 Tbl. minced shallots
2 lbs. ripe tomatoes, peeled and diced (see Before Beginning)
1 Tbl. fresh thyme leaves
salt and pepper
strips of lemon peel to garnish
fresh chervil to garnish

1. Lay the salmon fillet skin side down on a cutting board. Using a very sharp knife, slice the salmon into eight to 10 thin scallops at a 30-degree angle. Discard the skin.

2. Coat a baking dish with olive oil.

3. In a small mixing bowl, combine the crème fraîche and mustard. Coat the salmon scallops with this mixture and place them in the oiled baking dish. Cover and refrigerate.

4. For the sauce, heat the olive oil in a small skillet. Add the garlic and shallots and cook over low heat until tender. Add most of the tomato, reserving some for garnish, and the thyme. Cook over moderately-high heat, stirring until most of the moisture has evaporated and the mixture is thick. Purée in a food processor or blender. Add salt and pepper to taste.

5. About 15 minutes before serving, preheat the broiler. Broil the salmon for one to two minutes on each side. Place a little sauce on each warm plate and lay one or two salmon scallops atop the sauce. Garnish with lemon peel, some of the reserved tomato and chervil.

*TIPS

—Crème fraîche can be found in gourmet markets, or you can make your own by blending one cup of heavy cream with two tablespoons of buttermilk in a glass jar. Cover and let it stand at room temperature at least 12 hours and up to 24 hours. It should be very thick. Stir and store covered in the refrigerator. It should keep refrigerated for about 10 days.

—Moutarde de Meaux is mustard from the Meaux region of France. It is available in specialty markets. If you cannot find it, substitute a good coarse-grained Dijon.

Walnut-Crusted Baked Apples with Coriander Crème Anglaise

Serves: Eight

Adapted by Brett from a recipe by Michael Bortz of the Palmetto Grill in Denver, this is definitely comfort food.

1. Preheat the oven to 375°. Place the walnuts, sugar, cinnamon, nutmeg and coriander in a food processor and process until fine. Set aside.

2. Peel and core the apples and rub them with fresh lemon juice to prevent them from turning brown. Coat the apples with half of the melted butter, roll them in the walnut-spice mixture and place in a baking dish.

3. Mix the brown sugar, raisins and the four tablespoons of softened butter with a wooden spoon. Fill the center of

1 cup walnut pieces
½ cup sugar
1 tsp. cinnamon
½ tsp. freshly ground nutmeg
½ tsp. coriander
8 baking apples (McIntosh or
     Rome Beauty)
fresh lemon juice
1 stick unsalted butter, melted
½ cup packed dark brown sugar
½ cup raisins
4 Tbl. unsalted butter, softened
½ cup apple juice
Coriander Crème Anglaise
     (recipe follows)

each of the apples with this mixture and drizzle with the other half of the melted butter. Pour the apple juice into the bottom of the baking dish containing the apples and bake for one hour. Cool the apples for 15 minutes before serving. Serve with Coriander Crème Anglaise or cinnamon or vanilla ice cream.

Coriander Crème Anglaise

Makes: 2 cups

Serve this on the Walnut-Crusted Baked Apples. It's also quite good on other desserts, especially ones with apples. You can substitute other flavorings for the coriander, such as vanilla.

1½ cups milk (or half-and-half)
5 large egg yolks
⅔ cup sugar
1 Tbl. ground coriander

1. Place the milk in a heavy-bottomed, two-quart saucepan. Cook over medium-low heat until almost boiling.

2. Combine the egg yolks and sugar in a mixing bowl and beat with a whisk until well-blended and thick, but not bubbly. Gradually add the hot milk to the egg mixture, whisking constantly. Place the mixture back in saucepan.

3. Fill a large bowl with ice water. Cook the milk-egg mixture over low to medium heat, stirring constantly with a wooden spoon. If the custard begins to lump, put the saucepan in the ice water and whisk the sauce vigorously. When the custard coats the back of the wooden spoon, it is done. Stir in the coriander. Place the pan in the ice water and stir until the sauce has cooled. If not serving at once, store in the refrigerator.

Daily Bread

David Berenson, Chef/Owner

1738 Pearl Street,
Boulder
444-6549

*I*n the kitchen of Daily Bread you will find a 10,000-pound hearth oven from France that can hold 150 loaves of bread at once. "It's designed only for baking bread," says owner and chef Dave Berenson. "Only the French could be that passionate about bread." Maybe not. Berenson, himself, has some pretty strong feelings about bread.

It took Berenson a while to find his niche. His culinary training and experience has taken him from New Jersey to Colorado, California, Osaka, Japan, Massachusetts and back to Boulder, with a few stops in between. Berenson graduated from the Culinary Institute of America and did an extended internship in Aspen. He also baked for Pour La France while he was in Aspen.

Berenson was working at a beach restaurant in New Jersey when he met his wife Debbie. They both wanted a lifestyle, not just a life. "We fit everything we could into our Subaru wagon and went on a four-month road trip." Their last stop was Boulder. They arrived on July 4, 1985, and spent the evening in Chautauqua Park, drinking champagne and watching the fire works. And they stayed.

Berenson worked at Boulder Country Club as a sous-chef and later at Alfalfa's. He then accepted an offer from James Van Dyk (now chef-owner at The Greenbriar Inn) to be the chef at the Morgul Bismark. To this day, Berenson believes the Morgul was one of Boulder's best restaurants ever. When it closed, Berenson followed Van Dyk to the Santa Fe Bar and Grill in Berkeley, and Van Dyk followed Berenson to Japan when the grill closed. After two unhappy months in Japan, the Berensons returned to the States.

During his travels and through his experience in the food business, Berenson became increasingly interested in baking. Upon returning to Boulder, he became the chef at Marbles, and later returned to Alfalfa's, managing all of their food services. Berenson kept learning about the bread business, and in 1994, things fell into place for him. He found his present location on Pearl Street at the same time that the public began demanding better bread.

43

"People used to return from Europe and wonder why you could never find good bread here. There was really no good reason other than nobody had really tried in a meaningful way to make it. It involves equipment, technique, knowledge and lots of hard work."

Berenson believes that his biggest challenge is quality control. He is not the head baker at Daily Bread, Ian Duffy is. Berenson realized that in spite of his food industry background and his desire to make the product, he needed someone more knowledgeable: a real professional. When asked about his experiences since opening Daily Bread, Berenson admits, "It's been terrific and horrible and traumatic and rewarding – a real up-and-down experience. Then again, most of the good things in life are like that."

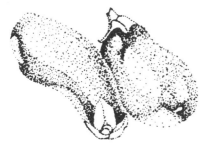

Famous Roasted Eggplant Sandwich

4 ½" round slices from a peeled medium eggplant
olive oil
salt and pepper
2 Tbl. freshly grated Parmesan cheese
4-6 dry packed, sun-dried tomatoes
2 slices olive bread
1 Tbl. roasted pepper, green or yellow, cut into thin strips (see Before Beginning)
1 Tbl. fresh basil leaves, cut into thin strips
2 oz. sliced mozzarella cheese
balsamic vinaigrette (see recipe on page 141)
1 slice red onion
red leaf lettuce leaves

Serves: One

This is one of the most popular sandwiches served at Daily Bread.

1. Preheat the oven to 375°. Lightly brush both sides of each eggplant slice with olive oil. Lightly season the slices with salt and pepper to taste and sprinkle them with the Parmesan. Place the eggplant slices on a baking sheet and roast, turning after five minutes, until browned; about 15 minutes. While the eggplant is roasting, soak the sun-dried tomatoes in water for 10 minutes, then cut them into thin strips.

2. Top one slice of the bread with roasted eggplant, roasted pepper, sun-dried tomatoes, basil and mozzarella. Season to taste with salt and pepper and drizzle with vinaigrette. Top with the onion and lettuce and the other slice of bread.

Panzanella (Italian Bread Salad)

Serves: Six as an appetizer or side dish

Panzanella is a delicious peasant salad from the Tuscany region of Italy. It makes a great side dish for grilled and roasted meats, and can also serve as a light lunch, appetizer or picnic food. Only hearty, chewy, country-style bread can stand up to the recipe's substantial flavors and juices. This dish needs to be made a day in advance so plan accordingly.

1. Slice the bread into ½"-thick slices. In a medium bowl, mix the tomatoes, capers, onion, cucumbers, ¼ cup of the olive oil and the vinegar. Add salt and pepper to taste.

2. In a shallow bowl or platter, alternate the sliced bread and the tomato mixture in layers, ending with the tomatoes. Cover and refrigerate overnight. Make sure the bread absorbs most of the tomato mixture's juices.

3. Just before serving, toss the salad with the basil and drizzle with additional olive oil. Add salt, pepper, vinegar and more olive oil to taste. Serve at room temperature or slightly chilled.

*TIPS
—Optional ingredients can include anchovies, olives, garlic, arugula, radicchio, parsley and celery.

½ loaf day-old hearty, chewy, country-style bread
3 tomatoes, peeled and cut into ½" pieces (see Before Beginning)
2–3 Tbl. capers
½ red onion, chopped
2 cucumbers, peeled, seeded and cut into ½" pieces
¼ cup olive oil, plus additional for drizzling
2–3 Tbl. red wine vinegar
salt and pepper
10 basil leaves, thinly sliced

Savory Bread Pudding

Serves: Six as a side dish or Four as a meal

"This is a terrific way to use leftover bread," says Berenson. "We like the way our Sundried Tomato Fougasse and our Pelopense Olive breads taste when baked into a custard." Serve the bread pudding as a side dish or with a salad for a luncheon dish or light supper.

1 Tbl. unsalted butter, plus more for baking dishes

1 medium onion, chopped or
    1 large leek, trimmed, cleaned well and chopped

1 tsp. fresh oregano, minced or
    ½ tsp. dried

¼ cup dry white wine or dry vermouth

salt and pepper to taste

3 cups milk

3 eggs, beaten

½-¾ of a loaf of stale, good bread, sliced into ½"-thick pieces*

2 cups grated mixed cheese, such as mozzarella, fontina, Parmigiano —experiment!

1. Preheat the oven to 375°. In a medium skillet, melt the butter. Add the onion or leek and cook over medium heat for five minutes. Add the oregano and wine and cook until the onion has softened and the liquid is almost gone. Remove the pan from the heat and season to taste with salt and pepper.

2. In a large bowl, beat the milk and eggs. Add a little salt and pepper. Butter a large baking dish (or individual ramekins). Line the baking dish with one layer of bread, trimming the bread to fit the container. Cover the bread with the onion mixture and then half of the grated cheese. Cover the cheese with another layer of bread and then the rest of the cheese. Pour the egg mixture on top.

3. Cover and bake for 20 minutes. Remove the cover and continue to cook until the custard is set and the top is golden brown (about 10-15 minutes).

*TIPS
—Use any good, coarse-textured bread. Breads with sundried tomatoes or olives are best. If using plain bread, add about ¼ cup of chopped sundried tomatoes and/or strong-flavored olives, layering them under each layer of cheese.

Dandelion Restaurant

Bob Allison, Executive Chef

1011 Walnut,
Boulder
443-6700

"*I*'ve been in the restaurant industry since I was 14—washing dishes back home in South Dakota," says Bob Allison, executive chef at Dandelion. Allison grew up on a farm where his family raised chickens, cows and pigs. They sold eggs and milk at the market. "We even churned our own butter in an old wooden churn because that's how Grandma did it," Allison says.

When he was eighteen, Allison moved to Denver, but he did not much care for big-city living. After two months and still without a job, he moved to Boulder. Allison's first job in Boulder was at the former L.A. (Last American) Diner. "It wasn't what I wanted," he admits. "I was a cook-fast hash cook – flip and go. I aspired for more."

The former Winston's Seafood Restaurant in the Boulderado Hotel was just what Allison was looking for. He learned plate presentation and cooking from scratch. When Winston's closed, he moved to Newport Beach, California, where he worked in one of the first "open kitchen" restaurants.

It was there that he realized he had found his niche. He claims he would work eighty hours a week and be totally content. Still preferring the small-town environment, however, he returned to Boulder after a year. By this time he had the training and experience to do something beyond flipping burgers.

Allison met Kevin Taylor, owner of Denver's acclaimed Zenith American Grill, at a conference where Allison was cooking. He had heard that Taylor was opening a restaurant in Boulder. "I asked Kevin what he thought of my food. I told him, 'This dinner is technically my resume. I want to work at Dandelion.'" Taylor was apparently impressed and welcomed Allison aboard. Within two months, Allison went from working chef to sous chef to head chef.

47

Allison draws inspiration not just from his restaurant experience but also from his roots, growing up on the family farm. He likes using products from local growers. The menu changes seasonally and the wines are specifically chosen to complement the food. Allison shares some delicious recipes that emphasize his belief that the simpler preparations are the best. "Cooking is a gift you give to others, but is also a gift to yourself because you enjoy what you're doing. It's not like work. I could do it forever."

Tuna Sashimi

Serves: Four

This is an easy appetizer that makes a colorful presentation with orange mango, green avocado and red tuna. Please note: the curry oil should be made at least 24 hours in advance, so plan accordingly. You will need cheesecloth for straining the oil.

For the curry oil:

1. At least 24 hours before serving, place all of the ingredients, except the olive oil, in a small skillet and toast over medium heat. Do not allow the spices to burn.*

2. Turn off the heat and add the olive oil. Blend well and store covered in a jar for at least 24 hours. Do not refrigerate. Strain the mixture through a cheesecloth and set aside until ready to use.

For the sashimi:

Divide the ingredients into four portions. On each of four chilled salad plates, alternate avocado and mango slices at the upper part of the plate in the shape of a fan. Arrange the tuna decoratively at the bottom of the fan. Place a dollop of wasabi at the lower part of the tuna. Squiggle the curry oil over the plate and sprinkle with sesame seeds. Serve at once.

*TIPS
—The point of heating the spices is to bring out their flavors. If you scorch them they will become bitter.
—Do not peel and slice avocados until just before using

½ tsp. cumin
¼ tsp. cayenne
1 ½ tsp. turmeric
1 tsp. coriander
½ tsp. ground ginger
½ tsp. allspice
½ tsp. black pepper
½ tsp. paprika
½ cup olive oil
1 avocado, peeled, seeded and thinly sliced just before serving*
1 mango, peeled, seeded and thinly sliced*
8 oz. sushi-grade tuna, thinly sliced
1 oz. wasabi paste*
curry oil in a squirt bottle* (see recipe above)
sesame seeds, lightly toasted

them or they will turn brown. Sprinkling them with lemon or lime juice will retard the browning process, but it will also alter the taste.

—Mangoes taste sweet with a little tart. Look for fruit with yellow skin blushed with red. If only green ones are available, place them in a brown paper bag to ripen. Mangoes are available from late spring to early fall.

—Wasabi is Japanese horseradish. It is the sinus-clearing "green stuff" served with sushi. It can be found in Asian and specialty markets and the Asian aisle of many groceries in paste or powder form. If you buy the powder, mix it with a little water or lime juice to make a thick paste.

—Squirt bottles can be purchased in stores carrying cookware, but a recycled plastic mustard or catsup bottle with a pointed tip works just as well.

Shaved Parma Salad

Serves: Four

You will love this unusual salad which proves Allison's theory that simplicity is best. The salad and dressing each contain just four ingredients – the result is delicious. Be careful not to overdress this delicate salad.

½ cup balsamic vinegar
2 Tbl. port wine
2 Tbl. dry red wine
2 Tbl. honey

For the Balsamico Dressing:
Combine all of the ingredients in a small saucepan. Cook over medium-high heat, stirring occasionally. When the dressing has reduced to a thick syrup, remove it from the heat and cool.

For the salad:

Toss the ham, fennel, figs and watercress together and add enough dressing to just moisten the ingredients. Add the olive oil and toss again. Divide the salad among four chilled plates and serve.

*TIPS

—Italian ham is called prosciutto. It is salt-cured and air-dried, and can be found raw or cooked. The prosciutto in Italian markets and specialty stores in the U.S. is most often cooked. The best prosciutto comes from Parma. If you substitute another type of ham the result will not be the same. Ask your butcher to slice it very thinly, then all you have to do is cut it into strips.

—Fennel is often called "anise. It's body looks like a leek's, while its leaves resemble dill's. For this recipe, use only the bulb; trim away the stalks and leaves as well as the root end. Cut the fennel in half vertically and thinly slice each half with the cut side of the fennel down.

—Dried figs can be found in specialty shops and some groceries.

—Before serving this salad, make sure the grocery has fresh watercress. It should be fresh looking with few wilted or yellowing leaves. Trim away any aged leaves before you store the watercress. Do not trim the stems. A good way to store watercress (and cilantro and parsley) is to wash it in cold water and place the stems in a glass of water like a bouquet of flowers. Cover the greens with a plastic bag and place them in the refrigerator until ready to use. Watercress usually only lasts for three or four days.

8 oz. Parma ham (prosciutto), thinly sliced and cut into strips*

4 small bulbs fennel, trimmed and thinly sliced*

12 dried figs, cut into strips*

1 large bunch of watercress, trimmed of wilted or yellow leaves*

1 Tbl. olive oil

Fillets of Salmon with Wine and Pepper Sauces

Serves: Four

Allison serves the salmon with lots of steamed fresh vegetables—baby carrots, zucchini, yellow squash, broccoli—and Smashed Yellow Potato Cakes (recipe follows). The sauce can be prepared up to two days in advance.

24 oz. salmon fillets
fresh lemon juice
salt and pepper
red and yellow pepper sauces
    (recipes follow)
lemon slices and minced Italian
    parsley for garnish

1. Season the salmon lightly with fresh lemon juice salt and pepper. You can pan fry, grill, braise, oven roast, broil, poach or steam the salmon.* While the salmon cooks, heat the sauces and finish the potato cakes.

2. To serve, spoon red pepper sauce on half of each of four very warm plates. Put yellow pepper sauce on the other half of each plate. Place a potato cake in the middle of each plate and arrange the salmon on top. Place the vegetables decoratively around the salmon and potato cake. Garnish with lemon slices sprinkled with the parsley. Serve immediately. Pass any extra sauce separately.

½ red bell pepper, seeds and
    white membranes
    removed, cut into 10 pieces
½ yellow bell pepper, seeds and
    white membranes
    removed, cut into 10 pieces
1 cup dry white wine
½ yellow onion, trimmed and
    quartered
salt and pepper

For the sauces:
1. Using two small saucepans, place the red pepper in one saucepan and the yellow pepper in the other. Place ½ cup of wine and ¼ of the onion in each saucepan. Cover each saucepan and bring to a boil over medium-high heat. Lower the heat and simmer for 30 minutes, or until the vegetables are very tender.

2. Puree each mixture separately in a blender or food processor. Strain each through a very fine sieve. For each sauce you should have a smooth liquid which just

coats a spoon. Taste for seasoning and add salt and pepper as needed. Place the sauces in separate jars and store in the refrigerator if not using right away.

For the Smashed Potato Cakes:

1. Bring a large saucepan of lightly salted water to boil. Add the potatoes and cook them until tender, then drain and cool them. When the potatoes are cool enough to handle, peel them. Mash the potatoes in a bowl with the butter until they are somewhat lumpy. Stir in the chives and add salt and pepper to taste. Form the potatoes into four patties, or press into a ring mold, making four rounds. Cover and set aside until ready to saute.

2. About 15 to 20 minutes before serving, heat the olive oil in a large skillet. When the oil is hot, add the potato cakes and cook about eight minutes per side, until the patties are a deep, golden brown and hot throughout.

*TIPS

—The favored methods for preparing salmon seem to be braising, grilling, broiling, poaching and oven roasting. As a general rule, fish is done when it is no longer translucent, when you start to smell it and when the flesh feels firm and slightly springy. The theory of cooking fish until it flakes is an old wive's tale. If it is flaky, it is in fact probably overcooked. Pan frying preserves the taste of really fresh fish. Grilling adds a subtle, smoky flavor that compliments many varieties, like salmon. Poaching seals in the flavor and keeps the meat moist.

—If you cannot find Yukon Gold or Yellow Finn potatoes, you can substitute red-skinned potatoes, but the taste will not be as rich.

1½ lbs. Yukon Gold or
    Yellow Finn potatoes*
1 oz. fresh chives
1/4 cup butter room temperature
salt and pepper
1 Tbl. olive oil

Apple Napoleon

Serves: Six

This fun dessert will impress your friends. They'll never know how easy it is.

¼ cup pistachios, shelled and chopped
¼ cup sugar
pinch of cinnamon
pinch of nutmeg
½ box (½ lb.) phyllo pastry, thawed*
½ cup butter, melted

For the phyllo triangles:
1. Combine the pistachios, sugar, cinnamon and nutmeg and set aside.

2. On a flat surface place one sheet of phyllo (phyllo sheets usually come 12" x 17"). Brush the first sheet with melted butter using a pastry brush (or a new 1"-2" soft bristled paint brush). Top the first sheet with another and brush it with butter. Top with a third sheet of phyllo and brush it with butter.

3. After layering the sheets of phyllo, cut the sheets in thirds both lengthwise and widthwise; i.e. cut at 4" intervals lengthwise and just over 5½" intervals widthwise. You should have nine rectangles. Next, cut each rectangle on the diagonal into two triangles.

4. Sprinkle the top of each triangle with butter and sprinkle with the pistachio mixture. Place on a baking sheet and bake until golden, about 15 minutes. Cool and, if not using right away, store in a covered, air-tight container.

1½ cup sugar
3 Tbl. unsalted butter
¼ cup water
½ cup heavy cream
3 Granny Smith apples, peeled, cored and sliced

For the caramel sauce and apples:
1. Place the sugar, butter and water in a medium saucepan. Bring to a boil, stirring constantly, until the sugar dissolves and the mixture caramelizes, turning

golden brown. Add the cream and continue cooking and stirring until the mixture is smooth. Remove from the heat. Store, covered, until ready to use.

2. Place the apples and ⅔ cup of the caramel sauce in a medium saucepan. Cook, covered, over medium-low heat, stirring occasionally, until the apples are tender. Set aside.

For the whipping cream:
Combine all of the ingredients and whip until stiff.

½ cup heavy cream, very cold
1 Tbl. powdered sugar
⅛ tsp vanilla
fresh mint for garnish

To serve: On each of six dessert plates, place one phyllo triangle, top with a dollop of whipped cream and some caramel apples. Repeat the layers. Top with third phyllo triangle and spoon caramel sauce over the top. Garnish with fresh mint.

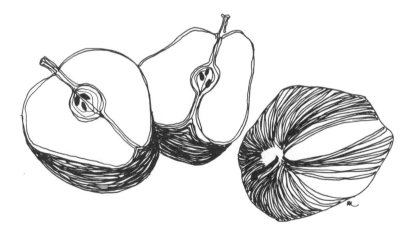

Dolan's Restaurant

Raymond C. Cunningham, Chef

2319 Arapahoe Avenue,
Boulder
444-8758

*M*ichael Dolan spent five months shucking oysters at Pelican Pete's in Boulder. Dolan claims he told himself then that he would own the building someday. When Pelican Pete's closed, several restaurants came and went attempting to make a go of it at the same location. The names and decor changed, but none of them lasted long. It almost seemed that there was a jinx on the place. Michael Dolan changed that.

Dolan and his brothers Geoff and Patrick opened Dolan's in 1994. The message on Dolan's menu reads: "Welcome to Dolan's Midtown Restaurant. A place where you can gather with old friends and meet new ones. Conduct business or escape from it. A place where we hope you will want to come back, time and time again." The message also says, "A place where your experience will include fine foods and great wines." They ensured the veracity of the latter statement by hiring Ray Cunningham to be their chef.

Cunningham studied business at Western Michigan University, and hotel and restaurant management at Michigan State University. His first real job as a chef was in 1978, when he was sous-chef at the Hilton Inn in Kalamazoo. He got plenty of experience working at the Hilton's two restaurants (which seated 275) and overseeing banquet facilities for 2,500. From there, he went to Lansing, Michigan, where he was executive chef for the Hoffman House Restaurant.

In 1987, Cunningham decided to move to Colorado. He took a sous-chef position at McCormick's Fish House in Denver. This is where he and Michael Dolan first met. Dolan was the manager of McCormick's. When Dolan realized his dream of owning a restaurant, he brought Cunningham along. "I did much of the ground work," says Cunningham. "I met with suppliers, created menus, developed order guides, worked with wait staff on menu knowledge ... and I made a commitment to see the restaurant develop into one of the best in the Boulder area."

Cunningham and the Dolan boys have proven a great combination. In addition to serving some of the best lamb in the county, they offer a variety of daily fish specials. Several (too often forgotten) pork dishes are also on the menu, such as pork tenderloin pan-fried with sliced apples and Gorgonzola, the recipe for which is included here. Among many great desserts is Dolan's signature multi-layered chocolate cake. However, no amount of begging could pry that recipe from Cunningham. He does share recipes for two appetizers and includes wine selections for each dish.

Yellowfin Tuna Quesadilla

Serves: Two as a first course
                 Four for cocktail nibbles

Cunningham recommends offering a Beringer White Meritage or an Antinori Orvie with this delicious appetizer.

¼ lb. yellowfin tuna Cajun or blackened fish spice blend*

2 (10") flour tortillas

¼ cup chopped mild green chilies*

¼ cup chopped roasted red bell pepper (see Before Beginning)

1 Tbl. + 1 tsp. minced fresh cilantro

6 oz. Monterey Jack cheese, shredded

¼ cup clarified butter (see Before Beginning)

fresh salsa*

cilantro sprigs to garnish

1. Season the tuna with the Cajun or blackening spices to your taste and set aside.

2. Place a 12" or larger skillet over medium heat. When the pan is hot, put in one flour tortilla and evenly spread half of the chilies, pepper and cilantro over it. Sprinkle the tortilla with half of the cheese.

3. While the cheese is melting, heat another skillet (cast iron works best) until very hot. Add the clarified butter. When the butter is quite hot, add the tuna and sear it on both sides. When the tuna is done to your liking, remove it from the heat (Cunningham prefers it rare to medium rare). Thinly slice the tuna into 16 pieces.

4. Repeat step 2 with the second tortilla. When the cheese has melted, divide the tuna and place it atop the melted cheese on the two tortillas. Cut each quesadilla into eight pieces. Place a small spoonful of salsa on each piece. Garnish with sprigs of cilantro and pass the extra salsa.

*TIPS

—There are many different kinds of Cajun or blackening seasonings. The *Boulder Cooks* test kitchen used Chef Paul Prudhomme's Magic Seasoning Blends Blackened Fish Seasoning. It does not contain MSG, sugar or preservatives, and is available at most groceries.

—Canned chiles are okay, though fresh are better.
—You should not use bottled or canned salsa in this recipe. To make your own salsa, combine to taste chopped tomatoes, minced garlic, chopped onion, minced green chilies or jalapeños (or both), chopped cilantro and fresh lime juice. Add salt and pepper to taste. If you do not want to make your own salsa, fresh salsas are available in many groceries and specialty stores.

Southwestern Chile Pepper Linguine

Serves: Four

This tasty dish is simple and fast. Serve it with a mixed green or spinach salad and a loaf of French bread. Cunningham recommends the Carmenet White Meritage or, if you prefer red wine, the Rocking Horse Zinfandel.

1. In a medium skillet, heat two tablespoons of the olive oil over medium-high heat. Add the shrimp and cook for three minutes, stirring often.

2. Add the mushrooms, jalapeños, red pepper and garlic. Cook for another three or four minutes, stirring often. Add the cilantro and sherry. Simmer for a few minutes, until the shrimp are cooked through and pink. Add salt and pepper to taste.

3. Toss the linguine with the one tablespoon of olive oil. Add the shrimp mixture to the linguine and toss. Place in warm pasta or soup bowls and serve immediately.

2 + 1 Tbl. olive oil
1 lb. rock shrimp, peeled and
   deveined
½ cup sliced mushrooms
2 jalapeño peppers, carefully
   seeded, veins removed and
   minced (See Before
   Beginning)
½ cup finely chopped red bell
   peppers
2 garlic cloves, minced
2 Tbl. chopped fresh cilantro
1 cup sherry
salt and pepper
1 lb. cooked chile pepper
   linguine, drained

Pork Medallions with Gorgonzola Cream Sauce

Serves: Four

A Dolan's favorite. Cunningham recommends the Hess Collection Chardonnay or Acacia Pinot Noir. Serve the pork with wild rice or orzo cooked in chicken broth with a little minced shallot.*

2 pork tenderloins (about
      2 lbs. total)
salt and pepper
flour
4 Tbl. olive oil
2 red apples, cut into wedges
      (peeled if desired)
½ cup dry white wine
1 cup heavy cream
4 oz. Gorgonzola cheese
salt and pepper

1. Slice the pork into 1½" thick rounds. Slightly pound the slices to flatten them into medallions. Lightly season the pork with salt and pepper and then dredge it in flour. Heat the olive oil over medium heat in a large skillet, then add the medallions in batches. Brown the medallions on both sides, setting each batch on a platter covered with foil when they're done.

2. When all of the pork is cooked, add the apples and wine to the skillet. Bring to a boil and then reduce the heat and simmer until the apples are cooked.

3. While the pork is cooking, pour the cream into a small saucepan and bring it to a boil. When it has reached a rolling boil, stir in the Gorgonzola. Continue stirring until the cheese has melted and the mixture is smooth. Simmer until the mixture thickens to a gravy-like consistency. Add salt and pepper as needed.

4. To serve, place a large dollop of Gorgonzola Cream Sauce on each of four warm plates. Divide the medallions among the plates atop the cream. Top the pork with the apples. Spoon the rice or orzo beside the pork along with your choice of vegetable. Drizzle the pork with a little more cream and serve. Pass the remaining Gorgonzola cream separately.

*TIPS

—Orzo is a small rice-shaped pasta that is a great sub-stitute for rice. To prepare it, fill a saucepan with equal amounts of water and broth, and bring the mixture to a boil. Add the orzo and boil for approximately 15 minutes, or until al dente. While the orzo is boiling, cook some minced shallots or onion in some butter or oil. When the orzo is finished, drain and toss with the shallot and butter mixture. Add salt and pepper to taste. 1½ cups of uncooked orzo serves four.

Fast Eddie's

Eddie Ermoian, Chef/Owner

Pearl Street Mall, Boulder

*E*ddie Ermoian has fulfilled a life-long dream. "Other kids wanted to be cowboys or policemen or firemen or something, but I wanted to run a hot dog stand." Ermoian grew up in Chicago one mile north of Wrigley Field, home of the Chicago Cubs. "I went there every day there was a game, since I was about eight. My knuckles are still sore and red from climbing the chain link fence at Waveland Avenue to get into the ballpark."

Ermoian's grandfather had two friends who manned hot dog stands on opposite sides of the park. Ermoian would walk up to one of them and stand with his lower lip hanging out. The owner would ask if he wanted a hot dog. He grins, "Then I would race like hell to the other stand and get him to give me a hot dog. I did this three or four times a game and they never did figure out what I was doing."

Ermoian spent 40 years working for Anheiser Busch. He relocated his family five times, ending up in California. After 16 years on the Monterey Peninsula, he decided to take early retirement. "One of the problems with relocating so many times is that you never get to live close to family," he explains. He and his wife Nancy both came from large families, so there were many places they could live that would be near relatives. Boulder County proved the most appealing, and they bought a house in Lafayette.

In pursuit of his lifelong dream, Ermoian opened Fast Eddie's, first at the Farmer's Market in Boulder and then at a location on the Pearl Street Mall in front of the Boulder Courthouse, where you now find his trademark sign, "Chicago Spoken Here." He is open seven days a week, weather and disposition permitting.

Ermoian shares his hot dog recipe and the secret to the popular, savory cucumbers that accompany them, as well as some family favorites.

Fast Eddie's Chicago-Style Hot Dogs

Serves: One

This is the real thing! But, unless you have relatives or friends in the Chicago area, you will have to see Eddie for the ingredients. He has a "Fast Eddie's Do It Yourself Party Pack" that includes all the fixins' plus napkins, waxed paper and a Fast Eddie's apprentice hat. The party pack serves ten, with one hot dog per person.

1. Sprinkle the cucumber spears with celery salt (that's the secret!).

2. Steam the poppy seed bun. Place a cooked, pure beef Vienna-style hot dog in the bun. Cover it with mustard, relish, sport peppers, onion, tomato wedges and a cucumber spear.

3. Enjoy the best hot dog ever!

1 cucumber spear
celery salt
1 poppy seed hot dog bun
1 pure beef Vienna-style hot dog
Chipico yellow mustard
Chipico sweet pickle relish
Chipico sport peppers
chopped white onion to taste
fresh tomato, cut into wedges

Beer 'n Cheese Soup

Serves: Four to Six

This soup is real comfort food. It's perfect for a cold Sunday evening in front of the fireplace or for company over to watch the game. Eddie likes to top it with a handful of unbuttered popcorn.

¾ cup shredded carrots
¼ cup chopped onion
4 Tbl. butter
¼ cup flour
1 12 oz. can Budweiser
2½ cups milk
8 oz. sharp cheddar cheese, shredded
salt and pepper
Tabasco Sauce
Worcestershire Sauce
fresh, unbuttered popcorn (optional)

1. In a large saucepan, cook the carrots and onion in the butter. When they are tender, add the flour and stir over medium-high heat for two minutes.

2. Add the beer and stir until the mixture begins to thicken. Add the milk and continue stirring until it is thoroughly blended. Simmer for 10 minutes, stirring occasionally.

3. Add the cheese a handful at a time, stirring until each addition has melted. Add salt, pepper, Tabasco and Worcestershire to your taste. Serve the soup hot, topped with a handful of popcorn.

TIPS
—For a thicker soup, use less beer; for a thinner soup, add more beer or milk.
—For those worried about fat content, use low-fat cheese, milk and butter, and light beer. However, these alterations will affect the soup's flavor.

Stuffed Grape Leaves (Dolmathes)

Makes: 30 dolmathes

Eddie serves these tasty appetizers with *Avgolemono Saltsa*, a lemon-egg sauce (recipe follows). Dolmathes make great "finger food" for a cocktail party or a Mediterranean dinner.

1. If using fresh grape leaves, place them in boiling water until they become limp; about 10 minutes. If using grape leaves from a jar, blanch them in boiling water for one minute and then drain them. Rinse with cold water.

2. In a medium-size bowl, combine the lamb, olive oil, onion, rice, parsley, tomato sauce, salt and pepper.

3. Place each grape leaf on a flat surface with the vein-side up and the smooth, shiny side down. Put approximately one tablespoon of the lamb mixture in the middle of each leaf (the amount will vary depending on the size of the leaf). Fold the stem end over the filling, then fold the sides of the leaf over the filling. Gently roll the grape leaf into a compact cylinder, starting from the stem end and rolling toward the leaf end.

4. Arrange the stuffed grape leaves in a heavy pot, one layer at a time. Place an oven-proof dinner plate upside-down on top of the last layer of Dolmathes to weigh them down.* Add enough chicken broth to come within ½" of the top of the last layer. Cover the pot and bring to a boil. Lower the heat and simmer until the dolmathes are tender, approximately one hour. The rice inside

50 fresh grape leaves
       (or 1 (16 oz.) jar of grape
       leaves), stems trimmed*
1 lb. ground lamb
1 Tbl. olive oil
1 medium onion, minced
⅓ cup long grain rice
       (uncooked)
¼ cup minced parsley
2 Tbl. tomato sauce
1 tsp. salt
½ tsp. pepper
2-3 cups chicken broth, more if
       needed

should be full and tender. Drain the dolmathes, reserving the cooking liquid for the sauce.

5. To serve, place the dolmathes on warm salad plates and drizzle with avgolemono sauce, or place them on a large platter with the sauce in a bowl in the middle.

*TIPS
—Fresh grape leaves are usually not commercially available so, unless you have a vineyard, you will have to buy grape leaves in a jar.
—The plate stays in the pot throughout the cooking. Its weight helps keep the dolmathes from unfolding.

Avgolemono Saltsa

---

3 large eggs, separated
juice of 2 lemons
¼ cup reserved hot cooking
    liquid from the dolmathes

Beat the egg whites until soft peaks begin to form. Add the yolks and continue beating. Add the lemon juice very slowly, beating constantly. Drizzle the hot, reserved liquid from the dolmathes into the sauce, beating constantly.

14th Street Bar & Grill

Alex Samir Aniba, Chef

1400 Pearl Street, Boulder
444-5854

*S*amir Aniba is a self-made man, or perhaps more accurately, a self-made chef. Aniba began as a dishwasher and prep cook in 1978 at the Caribe Hilton in San Juan, Puerto Rico. He first worked as an executive chef 10 years later. Today, he is executive chef at the 14th Street Bar & Grill. That's quite an accomplishment for someone who has no formal education in the culinary arts.

Aniba has worked mostly in the mid-Atlantic and southeastern United States; he worked his way down the seaboard from the Four Season's Hotel in New York to Washington, D.C., Virginia, North Carolina and Florida. He has been a prep cook, pantry cook, line cook, *saucier*, grill cook and banquet chef.

Aniba moved to Boulder in 1991 and has been at the 14th Street Grill ever since. He refers to himself as a "working chef." He says, "I do everything, from cooking to hiring and training staff, keeping track of inventory, ordering food, designing the menu and supervising the line."

Located on the corner of 14th and Pearl streets, the 14th Street B.A.G, as it is affectionately known, is a hip place to see and be seen. When the sun is shining, the best seats are outside, running along the west side of the restaurant, facing the mall for optimal people watching.

The grill's menu offers a variety of salads, sandwiches and pizzas, as well as more substantial fare, such as rotisserie chicken. The restaurant serves roasted turkey, stuffing, mashed potatoes and gravy, satisfying Thanksgiving cravings no matter what the season. While the set menu is consistently excellent, Aniba's creativity comes out in his Tunisian specialties.

Aniba proves that a passion for food and cooking can overcome a lack of formal training. Aniba attributes his love of cooking to his stepfather, a fellow restaurateur who influenced and educated the young Aniba. Aniba's

Tunisian grandmother also made a strong impression on his cooking style. Aniba contributed several Tunisian dishes to this volume: Berber-Spiced Lamb, Crispy Noodle Prawn, and Quail Egg and Crab Brik.

Grilled Asparagus and Chayote Salad

Serves: Four

This is a deceptively simple salad, first course or side dish.

1 lb. asparagus, blanched (see
      Before Beginning)
2 chayote, peeled and
      sliced ⅛"-thick*
salt and pepper

1. Season the asparagus and chayote with salt and pepper, using slightly more seasoning for the chayote.

2. Grill the vegetables over medium-high heat until they are just tender, turning at least once. Cut the chayote into strips. Divide the asparagus and chayote strips among four salad plates and arrange decoratively.

TIPS
—Also called mirlitons or vegetable pears, chayotes are a member of the squash family. They have a delicate flavor that has been described as a cross between an avocado and a zucchini. Chayotes are often stuffed and served as an entrée. They are pear-shaped and have pale green skin, and can be found in Latin markets and some groceries.

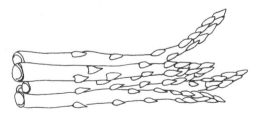

Quail Egg and Crab Brik

Serves: Six as an appetizer or first course

1. Place two to three tablespoons of crab in the middle of each of six lumpia wrappers. Crack one quail egg over the top of the crab and sprinkle with capers and parsley. Season with salt and pepper.

2. Moisten the edges of the lumpia wrappers with the egg wash. Fold the wrapper in half over the filling (forming a triangle or rectangle) and seal the outside edges by pressing them with your fingers or the prongs of a fork.

3. In a large, deep skillet, heat ¼" of oil over medium-high heat. Fry each brik until lightly browned and crisped on both sides. Serve on small plates garnished with lemon.

1 lb. crabmeat
1 package lumpia wrappers*
6 quail eggs*
¼ cup capers
1 bunch parsley, minced
salt and pepper
egg wash (1 egg beaten with 1 tsp. of water)
canola oil for frying
3 lemons, quartered lengthwise

*TIPS
—Lumpia wrappers are Philippine egg roll wrappers. You can substitute egg roll or won ton wrappers.
—Quail eggs are hard to find. You might be able to talk your local sushi bar out of a few, but if you can't find them, substitute chicken eggs. Use a scant tablespoon of beaten chicken egg for each quail egg.
—For smaller brik, use won ton wrappers. Put about one tablespoon of crabmeat in the middle of each wrapper and top it with one teaspoon beaten egg, a few capers and a sprinkle of parsley. Season the brik and then moisten the edges with egg wash. Fold the wrapper into a triangle and seal the edges. This will make a couple dozen mini-briks.

Crispy Noodle Prawns

Serves: Four as an appetizer

This is an unusual and delicious first course. Fresh pasta is wrapped around prawns and then deep fried. The prawns are served with a papaya coulis (purée).

2 ripe papayas, peeled, seeded
    and cut into chunks
2-3 red serrano chiles, carefully
    seeded and coarsely
    chopped*
1 Tbl. chopped gingerroot
juice of 1 lime
salt and pepper
4 large prawns
1 lb. fresh, uncooked pasta,
    such as angel hair,
    spaghetti or linguine*
canola oil for frying
sweet soy sauce*

1. To make the papaya coulis, purée the papayas, chiles and ginger in a food processor or blender. Add the lime juice and a little salt and pepper. Blend well. Set aside.

2. Wrap the prawns with fresh pasta, overlapping the strands. In a large saucepan, heat about 4" of oil to 370°. Fry the pasta-wrapped prawns in the oil until golden brown and crispy, making sure the prawns are cooked. Do not crowd them in the pan. Fry them one at a time if you have to. Drain on paper towels.

3. To serve, ladle a pool of the papaya coulis in the middle of four plates. Place the prawn in the middle of the pool and decoratively drizzle sweet soy sauce around the plates.

*TIPS
—Use two or three serrano chiles, depending on how spicy you like the coulis. If you cannot find red serranos, use green chiles or chile paste to taste.
—Variations in pasta size and color will enhance the presentation and add different flavors.
—Sweet soy sauce can be found in Asian markets and some groceries.

Berber-Spiced Rack of Lamb

Serves: Two

The flavor of this dish is wonderful and it is very simple to prepare. It makes an impressive presentation and the recipe can be easily multiplied if you are having guests. Aniba suggests serving the lamb with couscous, rice or bulgar wheat and grilled vegetables. A hearty red wine, such as a Zinfandel or big cabernet, goes well with the lamb. Aniba roasts the spices whole and then grinds them in a coffee grinder.

1. Combine the cinnamon, coriander, cumin, rosemary, cardamom, garlic, pepper and salt, and mix well. Thoroughly rub the spice mixture all over the lamb.

2. Preheat the oven to 425°. Heat the olive oil in a sturdy roasting pan over high heat and then quickly brown the lamb on all sides. With the rounded side (or the fat side) up, spread the harissa sauce over the lamb. Dust it with a little flour and snugly wrap the lamb in aluminum foil. Roast the lamb for approximately 20 minutes, until it's rare to medium-rare, or done to your taste.

3. Remove the lamb from the oven and let it sit for a minute or two. Slice between the ribs and arrange the chops on warm plates.

*TIPS
—Ask your butcher for a frenched rack of lamb (one with the meat cut away from the bone to expose the end of the bone). Many markets have them readily available

1½ tsp. cinnamon
1 Tbl. ground coriander
1 Tbl. ground cumin
3 Tbl. chopped rosemary
1 Tbl. cardamom
4 Tbl. minced garlic
1 Tbl. pepper
2 tsp. salt
1 rack of lamb, trimmed so that
     the rib bones are exposed*
3 Tbl. olive oil
1 cup harissa *
flour

in the meat section. If you are having company, get one rack of lamb for every two people. Make 1½ recipes of the spices and harissa for four people and double the recipe for six.

—Harissa is a Tunisian sauce of hot chiles, garlic and spices. It can be found in cans and jars in Middle Eastern markets and other specialty markets, or ordered from catalogues specializing in hot sauces and chiles. If you are ambitious, Aniba includes the following recipe for harissa.

Harissa

1 large onion, peeled and quartered
2 carrots, peeled
2 garlic cloves, peeled
2-3 tomatoes, peeled and cored (see Before Beginning)
1 lb. spicy fresh red chile peppers (such as cayennes)*
juice of 1 lemon
¼ cup olive oil
1 tsp. ground coriander
1 tsp. ground cumin
1 tsp. caraway
salt and sugar

Preheat the oven to 350°. In a large roasting pan coated with olive oil, place the onion, carrots, garlic, tomatoes and peppers. Cover the pan and roast until all of the the vegetables are soft. Skin and seed the chiles. Purée the chiles with the vegetables in a food processor. Add the lemon juice and ¼ cup of olive oil, coriander, cumin, and caraway. Add salt and sugar to taste.

*TIPS
—If you can't find fresh, spicy red peppers, use dried red chiles. Reconstitute the dried chiles by soaking them in warm water for 30 minutes.

A walk around Chet Anderson's farm starts in a large open barn where just-harvested produce is washed in huge sinks. Hanging upside down from the rafters are hundreds of drying flowers. Workers in the surrounding fields gather the ripe vegetables. A large greenhouse houses the winter crops. Next to Anderson's home is an absolutely delightful grape arbor, straight out of Italy. Inside the arbor, a wrought-iron table and chairs sit on a stone floor. "This is where we relax," explains Anderson. "It provides shade and even protects us from the winds."

Anderson grew up in Boulder, but not on a farm. His father was a heart surgeon. While in college, Anderson wrote a thesis on agricultural land preservation. "About 80 percent of the way through, I decided I wanted to be a farmer," he recalls. That was 1981. Today, he stocks restaurants, wholesalers and groceries with fresh produce. "Zolo Grill and Jax Fishhouse feature our greens and call them 'Chet's Greens.'"

The types of crops he grows change annually. "For example, next year you won't see tomatoes or eggplant. We'll probably do more greens instead. They grow fast, everybody needs them and we can keep turning them over." Anderson is always aware of what is 'in' and adjusts his crop mix accordingly.

Many factors affect business besides the weather. The latest food fads have a great influence on demand for a particular crop. Even a front-page spread in the food section of the newspaper can affect the buying habits of consumers. If a particular vegetable is not selling, Anderson gives samples to the restaurants. "For example, I will go to local chefs and say, 'Hey, these pumpkins are really great and here is what you can do with them.' Then I leave a box of pumpkins and let the chef play around with them."

Anderson doesn't just grow vegetables and herbs.

The Fresh Herb Company

Chet Anderson, Owner

4114 Oxford Road, Longmont
449-5994

Much of his crop is devoted to flowers, which he sells at the Boulder and (Denver's) Cherry Creek farmer's market, as well as to a limited number of wholesalers. Anderson also sells flowers out of the barn. The choices available depend on what is blooming at the moment.

The Perfect Vinaigrette

Makes: approximately 2 cups

"This is one thing nobody seems to be able to make. People call me all the time asking me to make it. First of all, you have to use the best products: extra virgin olive oil and the best balsamic vinegar you can find. For a slightly sharper tasting dressing, use three parts oil to one part vinegar; if you like it less sharp, use four parts oil to one part vinegar." (The following recipe is made with the three to one ratio of oil to vinegar.)

4 shallots, minced
1 tsp. salt
½ cup balsamic vinegar
1½ cups extra virgin olive oil

In a bowl or jar, combine the shallots, salt and balsamic vinegar, and stir the mixture until the salt has dissolved. Add the oil and beat the dressing with a whisk or shake it in a jar. Toss the dressing with fresh greens.

*TIPS
—For raspberry vinaigrette, crush overripe raspberries and strain the juice (to taste) into the basic vinaigrette.
—Toasted pine nuts or other nuts are delicious with the vinaigrette. Other additions could include roasted peppers or different cheeses such as feta or Gorgonzola.
—Try using this dressing on a Greek salad with feta cheese, kalamata olives, cucumber, dried oregano, tomatoes and red onion.

Pumpkin Stuffed With Parmesan Risotto

Serves: Four as an appetizer or Two as an entree.

This is one of Anderson's all-time favorites. It makes a very interesting and impressive presentation.

1. Preheat the oven to 425°. Cut off the top of the pumpkin (like you would a jack-o'-lantern). Scoop out the soft, seedy pulp. Invert the pumpkin in a baking dish filled with a few inches of water. Bake the pumpkin until tender, but not mushy; approximately 20 to 30 minutes (the cooking time depends on the size of the pumpkin).

2. While the pumpkin is baking, prepare the risotto. Heat the butter or oil in a large skillet (at least 10" in diameter). Add the onion and cook them until soft, stirring occasionally. Add the rice and cook, stirring, until the rice is glazed or translucent. Add the currants (optional) and then the hot broth, ¾ cup at a time, stirring often. As soon as each addition of broth is absorbed, add the next ¾ cup and repeat until all of the broth has been absorbed. The rice is done when it is al dente and has a creamy texture, with most of the liquid absorbed (see Before Beginning). Add the Parmesan and mix thoroughly. Add salt and pepper to taste.

3. Place the vinegar in a small saucepan and boil it until it is the consistency of syrup. Place approximately half of the balsamic syrup in the bottom of the pumpkin. Spoon the risotto into the pumpkin, mounding it at the top. Drizzle the remaining balsamic syrup over the risotto

1 small (1-1½ lbs.) pie pumpkin
1 Tbl. butter or oil
½ cup chopped onion
1 cup Arborio rice (see Before Beginning)
¼ cup dried currants, soaked in a little white wine for 10 minutes to plump (optional)
2½-3 cups hot chicken or vegetable broth
¾ cup freshly grated Parmesan cheese
salt and pepper
1 cup balsamic vinegar
green herbs to garnish, such as thyme and oregano

and garnish it with a few sprigs of green herbs. To serve, cut the pumpkin into fourths for an appetizer or in half for an entree. Eat the risotto and the pumpkin flesh.

Steamed Green Beans With Shiitakes and Cheese

Serves: Four to Six as a side dish

"The best vegetable recipes are the simplest," states Anderson.

1-1½ lbs. fresh green beans*
2 Tbl. butter
¼ lb. shiitake mushrooms, cleaned, stemmed and sliced
¾ cup grated Oka cheese*
salt and pepper

1. Snap off the ends of the beans and place them in a steamer over lightly salted, boiling water. Cover the pot and steam the beans until done to your liking; about 10 minutes for crispy-tender beans (see Before Beginning).

2. While the beans are steaming, heat the butter in a small skillet. When the butter is melted and bubbling, add the mushrooms and cook until tender; about 10 minutes.

3. Drain the beans and place them in a warm bowl. Add the mushrooms and cheese, and toss. Add salt and pepper to taste. Serve immediately.

*TIPS
—Choose bright green beans of a uniform size. The smaller the beans are, the more tender they will be. They should "snap" when bent.
—Oka is a Canadian cheese with a medium-strong taste and the consistency of a semi-hard cheese, such as fontina. It can be found at specialty markets and some groceries.

Grilled New Potatoes and Greens

Serves: Six as an appetizer or side dish

The potatoes may be roasted in a very hot oven, but the best way to cook them is to grill them over very high heat. However, if you roast them in the oven they do not have to be parboiled first. We have included a recipe for Don's Killer BBQ Potatoes on page 78. It uses new potatoes prepared in the same manner as Anderson's, but basted with a zesty barbecue sauce.

1. Fill a large saucepan with lightly salted water and bring to a boil. Add the potatoes and boil for about 10 minutes. The first ¼" of the potatoes should look cooked when halved. Drain.

2. Grill (or roast) the potatoes over very hot coals, turning often, until a crust has formed on the outside and they are tender inside.

3. While the potatoes are grilling, place the Gorgonzola in a large bowl. Divide the arugula among six salad plates. When the potatoes are done, add them to the Gorgonzola and toss. Add salt and pepper to taste and serve immediately.

2-2½ lbs. small, red-skinned, new potatoes, washed and trimmed as necessary
½ lb. Gorgonzola Dolce cheese, plus more to taste*
4 cups arugula, washed
salt and pepper

*TIPS
—Gorgonzola Dolce is a slightly sweet, softer variety of Gorgonzola. It can be found at specialty markets.
—Use the smallest red-skinned potatoes available. If only larger ones are available, quickly halve them before tossing them with the cheese.

Don's Killer BBQ Potatoes

1 medium onion, chopped
2 Tbl. olive oil
1½ cups ketchup
½ cup brown sugar
1 tsp. salt
½ tsp. dry mustard
3 large garlic cloves, minced
1½ cups water
1 Tbl. Worcestershire Sauce
¼ tsp. Tabasco Sauce
¼ tsp. cayenne pepper
2 tsp. Liquid Smoke
1 tsp. cider vinegar
½ tsp. black pepper

Combine all of the ingredients. Follow step 1 in the preceding Grilled Potato recipe. Before going on to step 2, coat the potatoes with Don's Favorite BBQ Sauce. While the potatoes are cooking, generously baste them with more of the sauce. When the potatoes are done, quickly halve or quarter them and place them in a large bowl. Toss with butter, salt and pepper.

"Some people's food always tastes better, even if they are cooking the same dish, because one person has much more life in them—more fire, more vitality, more guts—than others."

—*Rosa Lewis*

Full Moon Grill

Bradford Heap, Chef/Owner

2525 Arapahoe Avenue,
Arapahoe Village
Shopping Center,
Boulder
938-8800

*T*asting one of Bradford Heap's dishes, you will understand Rosa Lewis' above quote; his food has a vitality that is rarely found in the average restaurant. Heap, co-owner and chef of the Full Moon Grill is a perfect example of the new breed of passionate young chefs making Boulder County their home.

Heap can't remember a time when he was not interested in food. He grew up in Boulder and worked in several restaurants around town, and then in Napa Valley. He studied at the Culinary Institute of America and also studied for 14 months in France and Italy. When he returned to Boulder in 1993, he signed on with the Pearl Street Inn, a bed and breakfast, but not a restaurant open for dinner. Heap changed that by offering a limited but thoughtful dinner menu and established a reputation as an exceptional chef in just one year.

What he really wanted, however, was a place of his own. The Full Moon Grill had been open about two years when Heap and founder Rick Stein joined forces in 1994. Heap's food demonstrates the influences of his work and studies in Europe. A favorite appetizer is pear and grilled polenta in a Gorgonzola sauce. The Full Moon Grill serves a variety of pastas and a risotto special each day. Fish, grilled meat and poultry dishes are also available, such as grilled free range chicken breast with garlic mashed potatoes in a portobello mushroom sauce. Heap's desserts excel as well, particularly the tiramisù. With layers of mascarpone cheese, chocolate and sponge cake dipped in coffee, it is an exceptional example of this traditional Italian dessert.

Heap changes the menu often, planning around seasonal vegetables and fruits. Oils infused with flavor and oven-dried tomatoes are not purchased but come from the restaurant's kitchen. Heap believes that eating good food should be a sensual experience. "Cooking is a celebration of life," Heap says. "I want my customers to enjoy the food that we prepare with good friends, good wine and good conversation."

Crispy Polenta with Grilled Pears in Gorgonzola Cream

Serves: Four as an appetizer or light entrée (plus leftover polenta)

1 medium onion, finely minced
2 Tbl. extra virgin olive oil
1 cup polenta
4 cups water
salt
canola oil
½ cup heavy cream
4½ oz. Gorgonzola cheese, plus more as needed
2 medium pears,* halved and cored
2 oz. pine nuts, toasted
chopped Italian parsley to garnish
chopped red bell pepper to garnish

1. Preheat the oven to 350°. Place the onion and olive oil in an oven-proof saucepan and cover. Cook the onions over low heat for about five minutes, until tender but not browned. Add the polenta and stir for one minute (this sears the polenta). Add the water, and salt to taste. Bring to a boil, stirring constantly. Immediately remove the pan from the heat and cover.

2. Place the pan in the oven and bake for about one hour, stirring after 30 minutes. The mixture should be smooth. Oil a 10"x10" baking dish and pour the polenta into it. Smooth the top and let it cool. The polenta can be made to this point up to two days in advance.

3. Cut the polenta into eight small rounds, squares or triangles.* Place a little canola oil in a skillet and heat

until the oil is almost smoking. Add the polenta rounds to the pan and sear until each side is golden brown.

4. To make the sauce, heat the cream to boiling and transfer it to a blender along with 4½ oz. of the Gorgonzola. Blend until smooth. If the mixture seems too thin, add more Gorgonzola to thicken it.

5. Cut a 45-degree angle slice from the back of each pear half so they will sit up on the plate. Lightly brush each pear half with canola oil and grill (or bake at 400°) until heated through. Be careful not to cook the pears too long or they will become mushy.

6. To serve, put a little sauce on a warm plate. Place two rounds of pan-fried polenta on the bottom part of the plate and place one grilled pear half at the top. Sprinkle with pine nuts and serve. For more color, sprinkle with chopped Italian parsley and/or a small amount of diced red bell pepper.

*TIPS
—Cookie cutters work well for cutting the polenta.
—Heap recommends Comice pears, but Bosc pears work as well. They should be ripe and unblemished. If ripe pears are unavailable, try placing unripe ones in a brown paper bag with some bananas and let them sit for a day or two. If you are getting the pears ready to cook, but are not cooking right away, rub the pear halves with a little fresh lemon juice so they don't turn brown.

Italian Risotto with Fennel, Tomato and Shrimp

Serves: Four

4 Tbl. extra virgin olive oil
1 large onion, finely minced
1 small fennel bulb, cored and
    thinly sliced
1 garlic clove, minced
1½ cups Arborio rice (see
    Before Beginning)
¾   cup dry white wine
1 (8 oz.) bottle Doxee clam
    juice
5 cups low-sodium chicken or
    vegetable stock
4 Roma tomatoes, peeled and
    chopped (see Before
    Beginning)
2 Tbl. grated Parmesan cheese,
    plus more as needed
20 uncooked medium shrimp,
    peeled and deveined
salt and pepper

1. Place two tablespoons of the olive oil in a stainless steel saucepan. Over medium heat, add the onions and fennel, cover and sweat until soft (see Before Beginning). Do not allow the onions to brown. Add the garlic and rice. Cook for one minute, stirring constantly.

2. Add the white wine and cook, stirring often, until the wine has absorbed into the rice. Add the clam juice and cook, stirring often, until the juice has absorbed. Add the stock ½ cup at a time, stirring after each addition, until the liquid has absorbed. This should take about 30 minutes at mile-high altitude. The rice should be al dente and very creamy (see Before Beginning).

3. Stir in the tomatoes and Parmesan. Simmer over medium heat until most of the liquid has absorbed and the risotto is smooth and creamy. Season with salt and pepper.

4. For the shrimp, incise the back of the shrimp and devein. Season lightly with salt and pepper. Just before you are ready to serve, place two tablespoons of the olive oil in a skillet over high heat. When the pan is very hot, add the shrimp and cook for one minute on each side. The shrimp should be pink and just opaque inside.

5. Divide the risotto among four warmed pasta bowls and top with the shrimp. Sprinkle with extra Parmesan and serve immediately.

Penne Pasta Primavera

Serves: Two

You do not boil the pasta first.

1. In a large saucepan, heat the olive oil over medium heat. When hot, add the pasta and vegetables. Pour in enough chicken broth to just cover the pasta (approximately three cups). Add the salt, pepper and thyme.

2. Bring the mixture to a boil over high heat, then lower the heat, cover the pan and simmer for 25 minutes (at mile-high altitude), stirring after 15 minutes.

3. Taste the pasta to test for doneness; it should be slightly underdone. Stir in the basil and simmer, covered, for another two minutes. Remove the cover and turn up the heat. Cook until the juices thicken slightly. Remove from heat, stir in the Parmesan and butter. Divide the pasta between two heated plates and season with pepper to taste. Pass extra Parmesan.

TIPS
—If you include artichokes, be sure to rub them with fresh lemon juice after trimming to keep them from turning dark.
—To trim an artichoke, pull off the outside leaves. Cut off the end of the stem leaving about 2". Scoop out the choke (the fuzzy center) with a spoon (a grapefruit spoon works well). Trim away the remaining fibrous outer layer of the artichoke and pare away the tough outside skin from the stem. What you have left is the heart of the artichoke.
—More fresh herbs may be added, if you like.

3 Tbl. extra virgin olive oil
½ lb. penne pasta
1 medium onion, coarsely
        chopped
4 green onions, trimmed and
        sliced ½"-thick, including ⅓
        of the green tops
1 green bell pepper, coarsely
        chopped
2 artichokes (optional), with
        leaves, choke and tough skin
        around the heart removed,
        or ½ can (more or less to
        your taste), unmarinated,
        artichoke hearts, chopped
3 large tomatoes, peeled, seeded
        and roughly chopped (see
        Before Beginning)(or 1
        (14 oz.) can chopped
        tomatoes, including juice)
2 cups chicken broth (or
        veggie broth for a vegetarian
        dish), plus more if needed
½ tsp. each salt and pepper
1 Tbl. minced fresh thyme (or 1
        tsp. dried)*
1 Tbl. minced fresh basil (or 1
        tsp. dried)*
½ cup freshly grated Parmesan,
        plus more for passing
2 Tbl. butter

The Greenbriar Inn

James Van Dyk, Chef/Co-owner

8735 North Foothills
Highway,
Boulder
440-7979

*T*he Greenbriar was started in 1967 by two German friends, Rudi Baeumel and Rudi Zwicker, who transformed a gas station into a gourmet restaurant. During the years "Big Rudi" and "Little Rudi" owned it, The Greenbriar was considered one of the best restaurants in the Boulder area. New owners James Van Dyk and Phil Goddard plan to bring the Greenbriar into the 21st Century with the same reputation for excellence.

The Greenbriar's original owners would not recognize the building today. The structure has been added onto in every direction, including up. Most recently, Van Dyk and Goddard brightened the main dining room by adding floor-to-ceiling French doors on the west side giving it an open feeling without sacrificing the basic charm of the room. Van Dyk has taken the same approach with the menu, lightening the food without loosing the great flavors.

Van Dyk is from Vermont. He attended the Culinary Institute of America and did his externship at Maxwell's Plum in San Francisco. Van Dyk first came to Boulder in the 1980s, at the beginning of a culinary renaissance in Colorado. Van Dyk was in the midst of it all.

He worked at the Morgul Bismark, which had the first wood-burning pizza oven in the state, and at the Blue Inn (now the 14th Street Bar & Grill), which introduced the open rotisserie to Colorado. It was there that he met his future partner, Phil Goddard. When the Blue Inn closed, he moved back to San Francisco and became executive chef at the Sante Fe Bar and Grill. A fire temporarily closed the restaurant and a restless Van Dyk took off for Europe. After several months of travel, he accepted a position with a large Japanese corporation as an executive chef. He was the first American chef to receive a work visa in Japan.

After four years in Japan, Van Dyk and his bride, a Japanese national, moved back to Boulder, where he was employed by Cliff Young's in Denver. During this time, he and Goddard renewed their friendship and began making plans for their own restaurant.

Van Dyk has great respect for his staff. In fact, he asked to give only one of his own recipes so that his chef de cuisine and his pastry chef could contribute as well. This ethos is reflected in Van Dyk's business motto, "My goal at The Greenbriar is not to educate the public. That's pompous. I want to satisfy the public."

Charred Tuna Fillet with Sweet Ginger-Lemon Butter

Serves: Four

Don't let the unusual ingredients in this dish discourage you; they can all be found at Asian markets, and the dish itself is easy and delicious.

1. Liberally season the tuna with togarashi seasoning and a little salt. Sear the tuna in a smoking hot skillet or on a very hot grill until done (medium is recommended).

2. Place the ginger, sugar and plum wine in a small saucepan and cook slowly until about ¼ cup liquid is left. Set aside until ready to serve.

3. Combine the Chardonnay and shallots in a saucepan and boil over high heat until the mixture reduces to about two tablespoons. Add the cream and boil until the mixture is thick. Off the heat, add the butter, in pieces, and stir until it has melted. Season with salt, pepper and fresh lemon juice to taste.

4 (4 oz.) yellowfin tuna steaks, #1 grade (sushi grade), cut as squarely as possible
2 Tbl. Japanese togarashi* seasoning
salt
6 oz. fresh ginger, peeled and cut into tiny strips
2 Tbl. sugar
½ cup Japanese plum wine
4 shallots, minced
1 cup Chardonnay
¼ cup heavy cream
1 stick of butter, cut into 8 pieces
salt and pepper
fresh lemon juice
1 small bottle Indonesian kecap manis*
1 head Belgian endive, cut into thin strips.
4 leaves obba shizo* (optional)
4 oz. tobiko caviar* (optional)

4. To serve, spoon the butter sauce onto four warm plates and drizzle decoratively with kecap manis. Place the tuna on top of the sauces. Sprinkle the border of the plate with the endive. Top each tuna steak with about one tablespoon of the ginger-plum wine mixture. Optionally, garnish the tuna with a leaf of obba shizo and a spoonful of tobiko caviar.

*TIPS
—Togarashi are small, hot, red Japanese chiles. They are also known as ichimi. This recipe calls for togarashi seasoning, not the peppers themselves. It can be found in Asian markets.
—Kecap manis or ketjap manis is an Indonesian sauce made with palm sugar and seasoned with garlic and star anise. It is somewhat similar to soy sauce, but thicker. An easy way to dribble the sauce is to place it in a recycled yellow mustard container with a pointed spout.
—Obba Shizo is a leaf that can be found in some Asian markets.
—Tobiko caviar is flying fish roe. It is available in Asian markets.

Quail Stuffed with Chanterelle Mushrooms and Spinach

Serves: Four

This delicious entrée is from Edward Schmidt, The Greenbriar's chef de cuisine. It is somewhat labor-intensive, but you will be very pleased with the result— it's delicious! Schmidt serves the quail with baby spinach and a hash of potatoes, celery root and butternut squash (recipes follow). He gently packs about ½ cup of the hash into a 2½" ring mold. He inverts the mold on one side of a warmed plate, then removes the mold, leaving a mound of hash. He places spinach on the other side of the plate. He then puts one quail on top of the hash and one on the spinach. He finishes the quail with a delicious roasted garlic sauce and a garnish of chives, leeks and candied garlic. You may have to order the quail and caul ahead of time from your butcher, so plan accordingly.

1. Heat two tablespoons of the olive oil in a skillet. Add the mushrooms and shallots and cook over medium heat for two minutes. Add the thyme and sage and continue cooking until the mushrooms are tender. Scrape into a large bowl.

2. Add another two tablespoons of olive oil to the skillet and place over high heat. When the oil is very hot, add the foie gras. Stirring constantly, cook until it is no longer pink. Add the cooked foie gras to the bowl containing the mushrooms. Add the spinach and almonds and blend well. Season with salt and pepper.

3. Stuff each quail with the mushroom mixture until plump. On a flat surface, cut the caul into squares big enough to wrap each quail. Place each quail breast-side-down and wrap with the caul. Season lightly with salt and pepper. Preheat the oven to 325°. In a large oven-proof skillet*, heat two or three tablespoons of olive oil. Over high heat, quickly sear the quail on all sides, starting with the seam of the caul down. Place the quail in the oven and roast for approximately 15 minutes. The quail should be slightly pink inside.

4. For the sauce, brown the reserved wing tips in a little olive oil. Add the onion, celery and carrot and cook until they begin to brown. Stir in the garlic purée and cook

For the quail:
6-7 Tbl. olive oil
½ lb. chanterelle mushrooms, sliced
¼ cup minced shallots
1½ tsp. minced fresh thyme
1½ tsp. minced fresh sage
8 oz. fresh foie gras, finely chopped*
2 cups cooked spinach, well drained and chopped
¼ cup sliced almonds, toasted
8 quail, wing tips trimmed and reserved
½ lb. caul*
salt and pepper

For the sauce:
Reserved wingtips
Olive oil
½ cup chopped onion
¼ cup chopped carrot
8 cloves garlic, roasted and puréed (see "roasting garlic" in Before Beginning)
1 quart brown chicken stock*
1 quart veal stock*
8 sprigs thyme
1 bay leaf
1 tsp. black peppercorns
salt and pepper
minced chives to garnish
leeks cut into strips to garnish
candied garlic (recipe follows)

for one minute, stirring. Add the stocks and bring to a boil. Add the thyme, bay leaf and peppercorns. Reduce the heat and simmer until the sauce has thickened. Add salt and pepper as needed. Garnish with minced chives, strips of leek and candied garlic.

*TIPS

—Foie gras is the liver of a goose (or duck) that has been overfed to produce an enlarged, fatty organ. Fresh foie gras is very expensive and difficult to find. You can substitute eight ounces tinned pâté de foie gras, found in specialty markets. If using fresh foie gras, try to find some that has been well cleaned (Otherwise, you must soak it for one hour in milk, then drain and rinse it with warm water. Separate the lobes and carefully split them. Remove all of the veins and ligaments.). Marinate the foie gras overnight in a mixture of ¼ cup Armagnac, ¼ cup Port and one teaspoon each salt, sugar and white pepper. When ready to use, drain and chop the foie gras for the recipe.

—Caul is a thin, fatty membrane that lines the abdominal cavity of pigs and sheep. Pork caul is the best. It looks like a fishing net and is used to hold foods like meatballs together or to wrap foods that tend to dry out. The caul melts away during the cooking process. It is not readily available and must be ordered in advance from the butcher.

—Brown chicken stock is made like regular chicken stock, except the chicken bones and vegetables are first roasted in the oven until browned.

—Veal stock is sold in some specialty markets. You can make your own or substitute one-half beef stock and one-half chicken stock.

—If you do not have an oven-proof skillet, transfer the quail to a cookie sheet before baking.

—Candied garlic can be found in specialty stores and gourmet markets. Or you can make your own (recipe follows.

Candied Garlic

Pull apart the heads of garlic and peel the cloves. Just barely trim the root end of each clove. Place the cloves in a saucepan with the butter, broth, sugar, salt and vinegar. Bring to a boil, then turn down the heat and simmer, covered, for about 30 minutes, until the garlic is tender. Remove the lid, turn up the heat and boil until the liquid is reduced, forming a glaze on the garlic. Stir often to coat each clove well. The garlic can be served hot or at room temperature. If you are not using the garlic right away, store it in a jar in the refrigerator.

2 whole pods (bulbs, not cloves) of garlic, carefully peeled, roots trimmed
2 Tbl. butter
¾ cup beef broth
2 Tbl. sugar
¼ tsp. salt
1½ tsp. sherry vinegar

Butternut Squash and Potato Hash

Serves: Four as a side dish

Edward Schmidt serves this with stuffed quail, but it goes well with many other dishes. It would be a perfect accompaniment for Thanksgiving turkey, for example.

1. Blanch the potatoes, celery root and squash separately in salted water until barely tender and then plunge in ice water to stop the cooking. Drain.

2. Heat the olive oil in a large skillet and add the onion and celery. Cover and cook over low heat until tender. Add the apples and continue cooking for one minute. Add the cooked potatoes, celery root and squash and cook until hot. Add the cinnamon and coriander, and salt and pepper to taste. Stir in the chives. Serve hot.

½ cup peeled, diced russet potatoes, cut in ¼" pieces
1 cup peeled, diced celery root,* cut in ¼" pieces
1 cup peeled, diced butternut squash, cut in ¼" pieces
3 Tbl. olive oil
¼ cup diced yellow onion
2 Tbl. diced celery
1 cup peeled, diced Granny Smith apples (about 2 apples)
1 tsp. cinnamon
1 tsp. ground coriander
salt and pepper
2 Tbl. minced chives

*TIPS
—Celery root is not the same as celery. It is brown with a very rough appearance. It tastes similar to celery, but stronger. Choose smaller roots with a minimum of knobs and bumps. Celery root can be eaten raw or cooked and makes a delicious salad.

Wilted Baby Spinach

Serves: Four as a side dish

Great with almost any entrée from pasta to roast beef.

6 cups baby spinach, stems removed (about 2 bunches)
1 tsp. pepper
¼ cup water
salt

Place a large skillet on high heat. Add the spinach and pepper and toss. Add the water and cover the pan. Cook for one minute, remove the lid and sprinkle with a small amount of salt. Serve as soon as possible.

Coconut Currant Flan

Serves: Eight

This mouth-watering dessert is from The Greenbriar's pastry chef, Luv Mills. She garnishes it with crispy somen noodles, which she forms into a fan and dusts with cinnamon-sugar.

1. In a bowl, gently mix the eggs and the yolks with a whisk (do not beat, creating bubbles). Add the vanilla, Grand Marnier and one cup of the sugar. Carefully stir with a whisk just to combine well (do not beat, creating bubbles).

2. In a large saucepan, eat the coconut milk, half-and-half and milk over medium heat until it is just ready to boil. Pour the hot milk into the egg mixture, stirring constantly. Strain this mixture through a fine sieve and then add the currants.

3. Preheat the oven to 275°. Place eight individual soufflé dishes or ramekins in a pan large enough to hold them all without touching. Heat water in a kettle for a water bath (see Before Beginning). Put the other 1½ cups of sugar in a heavy skillet and melt over medium heat, stirring constantly, until the sugar has caramelized and is a medium-brown color. Be careful not to burn it.

4. Divide the caramelized sugar among the ramekins and top with the egg mixture. Pour hot water in the pan with the ramekins to make a water bath. Cover with aluminum foil. Poke vents in the foil and place in the oven. Bake for approximately 90 minutes, until the

6 large eggs
6 large egg yolks
2 tsp. vanilla
2 Tbl. Grand Marnier
1 cup + 1½ cups sugar
1 (14 oz.) can coconut milk
1 cup half-and-half
1 cup milk
⅓ cup dried currants
cinnamon sugar (2 Tbl. sugar
    mixed with 2 tsp. cinnamon)
somen noodle fans to garnish
    (optional)*

custard barely wiggles. Remove from the oven and cool. (Do not remove from the water bath until cool.) Refrigerate until ready to serve.

5. To serve, run a knife around the sides of each ramekin and invert onto a plate. Dust with cinnamon sugar. Garnish with crispy somen noodle fans (optional).

*TIPS

—Somen noodles are thin, white noodles made from wheat flour. They can be found in Asian markets.
—To make crispy somen fans, heat 2" of canola oil to 370° in a heavy, deep pan. Beat one egg in a small bowl. Cut fresh somen noodles (or egg roll wrappers) into 3" strips. Arrange six to eight strips in a fan shape, flared on top and meeting at the bottom. Brush a little egg between each strip at the bottom of the fan and then press down on the strips to make them stick together. Fry the noodle fans in batches until crisp and golden brown. Drain on paper towels. Sprinkle with some of the cinnamon-sugar, cool and store in an air-tight container. If the fans come apart in the oil, try placing them between two flat metal spatulas or hold the bottoms of the fans with tongs while frying.

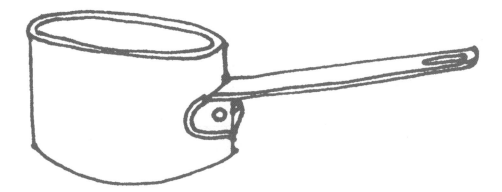

The Harvest

Mark Shockley, Manager

1738 Pearl Street,
Boulder
449-6223

Mark Shockley first worked in a restaurant at age 17, bussing tables at Phillip's Crab House in Ocean City, Maryland. "Phillip's seats about 1,000 people and does anywhere from 3,000 to 5,000 dinners a night," he says. "The best thing about working there was that they hired about 100 waitresses who were also about 17 or 18. I was much more into hanging out on the beach, meeting the waitresses and surfing than cooking back then."

When the owners of Phillip's opened a more upscale hotel and restaurant on the boardwalk in Ocean City, Shockley started bussing tables there. The owners of Phillips brought in a chef named Robert Lee from the Fountainbleau in Miami and Shockley and Lee became friends. Lee taught Shockley how to make ice carvings for the hotel's Sunday brunch buffet and by the end of the summer, Shockley was working as "a sort of assistant to the chef." He adds, "Some of the guys had worked in the business for years as breakfast cooks and dinner cooks and they taught me their old-style ways, whereas Robert taught me his newer ways. It was interesting and volatile at times, but lots of fun."

Shockley first came to Boulder in 1973 to house-sit for friends who were in South America for a year. In Boulder, he worked with Roger Berardi, who now owns Juanita's in Boulder and Denver and Berardi's in Denver. "Things were just beginning to happen when I got here," Shockley says. "It was dry until 1969, so the bar scene was starting to develop in the '70s." Shockley worked at Berardi's Gunbarrel Inn (now the Mockingbird on Lookout Road). When it closed in 1973, he approached Frank Day and Wayne Dozier, who had just opened The Walrus. "Frank was the next big influence on my life. I spent about eight years working with him and Concept Restaurants (which owns Old Chicago, Walnut Brewery and many other restaurants)."

Shockley wanted to get more involved with the food end of the business, so he left Concept Restaurants and went to Pelican Pete's, where he was in charge of catering. Much of their business involved people from the entertainment industry, leading to some wild stories: He had to supply sandwiches and a new, unused toilet for one singer, and M&M's with all of the red ones removed for another.

After running his own restaurant, Marbles, Shockley returned to Concept Restaurants for whom he now runs The Harvest. The Harvest features fresh, natural, healthful food. The menu reflects Shockley's love of cooking. "I have always loved food and loved people, and so the restaurant business is a natural for me. It's like having a party every night ... at someone else's house, and you don't have to do the dishes. It's great!"

Maple Walnut Vinaigrette

Makes   approximately 3 cups

This is Shockley's favorite salad dressing. It's very easy because the whole thing is done in a blender. A salad of fruit, nuts and cheese mixed with greens is great with it.

¼ red onion, cut into 4 pieces
1 garlic clove, coarsely chopped
1 egg yolk
½ cup champagne vinegar
½ cup maple syrup
1½ tsp. salt
½ tsp. white pepper
½ cup walnut oil
½ cup olive oil
½ cup peanut oil

Combine the onion, garlic, egg yolk, vinegar, maple syrup, salt and pepper in a blender or food processor. Blend until well mixed. Slowly add the oils while continuing to blend. Add more salt and pepper if needed.

Salmon Ceviche

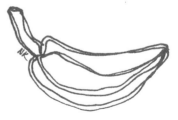

Serves: Ten to Twelve as an appetizer

An easy do-ahead dish that can be made the day before it is being served. It needs to be made at least six hours ahead so the citrus juices can "cook" the fish. Serve on crackers.

1. Remove any bones from the salmon and chop it into small pieces. Place the salmon in a glass bowl. In another bowl, mix the remaining ingredients and then pour them over the salmon. Cover and refrigerate the salmon for at least six hours.

2. Taste and add salt if needed. To serve, place the salmon in a decorative bowl surrounded by plain crackers such as Carr's Water Wafers.

1¼ lbs. salmon (or bay scallops)
juice of 4 lemons
juice of 5 limes
1½ tsp. pepper
¼ bunch cilantro, tops only, chopped
1 tsp. minced, peeled gingerroot
2 jalapeño peppers, seeded and minced
1 garlic clove, minced
1 tomato, peeled, seeded and chopped (see Before Beginning)
½ red onion, minced
½ tsp. red pepper flakes
salt, if needed

Bread Pudding with Blueberry Sauce

½ cup raisins
bourbon or rum
(optional)
1½ lb. stale loaf of unsliced
white bread
1 stick butter, melted
4 eggs
3 egg yolks
3 cups milk
¼ cup heavy cream
1¼ cups sugar
2 tsp. vanilla
½ lb. fresh or frozen blueberries
1 Tbl. fresh lemon juice

Serves: Six to Eight

1. Soak the raisins for one hour in enough bourbon or rum to cover (optional).

2. Preheat the oven to 350°. Cut the crust off of the bread, slice it thinly and brush butter on both sides of each slice. Overlap the bread slices in the bottom of a 10"x14" pan.

3. Beat the eggs and egg yolks. In a saucepan, heat the milk, cream and ¾ cup of the sugar. Stirring constantly, bring the mixture to a boil, then lower the heat. Add spoonfuls of the hot milk mixture to the eggs, whisking constantly, until half of the mixture has been incorporated. Pour the egg-milk mixture into the saucepan with the other half of the milk. Cook over low heat, stirring constantly with a wooden spoon, until the mixture has thickened slightly. Stir in the vanilla.

4. Pour the hot egg-milk mixture over the bread. Press the bread with a fork to make it absorb the mixture. Place the baking dish in a larger pan with hot water halfway up the sides. Bake for 45 to 50 minutes.

5. For the blueberry sauce, combine the blueberries in a small saucepan with ½ cup of the sugar and the fresh lemon juice. Bring to a boil over medium heat. Lower the heat and cook for two minutes. Cool before serving. Spoon the sauce over individual servings of the bread pudding and serve.

Taking a cooking lesson from Bruce Healy, you learn the right way to cook! Sloppy measuring is a no-no. Cutting corners is out of the question. Healy's recipes are not complicated, but they are precise. They are also clearly presented and understandable. It is easy to understand his attention to detail. Before turning to cooking, Healy was a physics professor.

Healy graduated Phi Beta Kappa from Williams College and holds a Ph.D. in theoretical physics from The Rockefeller University. He served on the faculties of The Institute for Advanced Study and Yale University, and has been published in numerous professional journals.

So, how did Healy get from writing articles such as "Model Independent Lower Bounds for Massless Particle Scattering" in a 1974 issue of *Physics Review* to "Mastering a Chocolate Fantasy Dessert with Bruce Healy" in the November 1986 issue of *Chocolatier*?

Healy and his wife Alice were living and working in Princeton, New Jersey. Alice's job as a psychology professor involved a fair amount of European travel and Healy often joined her. Visiting the pâtisseries of Paris was one of Healy's favorite pastimes, and he became fascinated with the art of making these delicacies. "My passion for French food eventually overwhelmed my interest in physics, and I gradually redirected all of my energies to teaching and writing about French cooking," he says.

Healy got to know and work with several of the most distinguished pastry chefs in Paris — Paul Bugat, proprietor of Paul Bugat Pâtissierie à la Bastille, in particular. He and Bugat collaborated on Healy's first book, *Mastering the Art of French Pastry*, which won an R.T. French Tastemaster Award for Cookbook Excellence and became "Recommended Reading" for *Food & Wine's* publication, *The Basics of Baking*.

During the time Healy was making the transition from physics professor to cooking teacher and author, he

Healy-Lucullus School of French Cooking

Bruce Healy, Owner/Cooking Instructor/Author

840 Cypress Drive, Boulder
494-9222

and his wife moved to Boulder. They loved the East, but now, having lived in Boulder since 1980, they are virtual natives. Their daughter, Charlotte, was born here in 1988. Alice is a professor at the University of Colorado and Bruce is working on his third cookbook.

Healy's second book, *The French Cookie Cookbook*, also co-authored with Bugat, was nominated for a James Beard Book Award in 1995. With this book, Healy takes the mystique out of baking these "edible jewels" and makes it fun, fast and easy. Therefore, we wanted some cookie recipes from him. Healy, however, insists that he is not just a baker and as evidence offers his simple but delicious beef rib-eye with shallot and vinegar sauce.

Entrecôte aux Échalote (Beef Rib-Eye with Shallot and Vinegar Sauce)

Serves: Six

Healy says, "I prefer the steaks *saignant*, which is French for 'very rare' or, even more literally, 'bloody.' I like to serve them with boiled new potatoes and a bottle of red wine from the northern Rhone Valley such as Hermitage or Côté Rotis. The sauce is best made with a mellow wine vinegar such as balsamic."

9 Tbl. unsalted butter (1 stick + 1 Tbl.), softened
6 beef rib-eye steaks, well trimmed
salt and pepper
4 medium shallots, minced
¼ cup red wine vinegar
2 Tbl. minced fresh parsley

1. Heat three tablespoons of the butter in a large skillet. When the butter just starts to brown, add the steaks and sear on both sides. Do not over cook; they are best rare to medium-rare. Transfer the steaks to hot plates and sprinkle with salt and pepper.

2. Add the shallots and vinegar to the same skillet and boil to reduce the vinegar slightly. Remove the mixture from the heat and whisk in the remaining six tablespoons of butter. Pour the sauce over the steaks and sprinkle with parsley.

Almond Lace Cookies

Makes: 25 to 30 cookies

1. Brush the edges and corners of three large baking sheets with melted butter and line each with parchment paper. Preheat the oven to 400°.

2. Cream the butter with a wooden spoon or in a mixer with the flat paddle. When it is smooth, light and creamy, sift in the sugar and beat until well combined. Add the egg and beat until well combined. Switch to a wire whisk or the wire beater and beat in the orange zest. Stir in the almonds with a rubber spatula. Sift the flour over the batter and fold in with a spatula.

3. Spoon the batter onto the prepared baking sheets using 2½ tsp. of batter per cookie. Arrange the cookies in staggered rows, separated by at least 2". Flatten each cookie with the back of a moistened fork to distribute the almonds evenly. Place one sheet at a time in the oven. Bake the cookies for seven to 11 minutes, until the cookies have spread and are brown around the edges, but still golden in the centers.

4. Place the baking sheets on wire racks to cool, then carefully remove the cookies with a metal spatula. The cookies should keep in an air-tight container for up to one week.

*TIPS
—Parchment paper can be found at some groceries and most cookery stores.

melted butter
parchment paper*
9 Tbl. (1 stick + 1 Tbl.) unsalted
    butter, softened
1 cup + 2 tsp. confectioners' sugar
1 large egg
zest of 1 orange
1 cup sliced almonds
¼ cup + 3 Tbl. flour

Raisin Boulders

Makes: 36 soft, almost chewy cookies.

The batter must be chilled overnight to produce the lumpy, boulder-like shapes.

6 Tbl. unsalted butter, softened
¾ cup sugar
3 large egg whites
1 tsp. vanilla
½ cup + 1 Tbl. seedless raisins
⅔ cup + 1 Tbl. flour
melted butter
flour

1. Beat the butter with a wooden spoon or the flat paddle of a mixer until it is smooth, light and creamy. Beat in half of the sugar. When smooth, beat in the remaining sugar followed by one egg white. Using a wire whip or the mixer's wire attachment, beat in the remaining egg whites, one at a time, and then the vanilla. Stir in the raisins with a wooden spatula. Sift the flour over the batter and mix it in with the wooden spatula. Cover the batter and allow it to rest overnight in the refrigerator.

2. Preheat the oven to 400°. Brush two or three large baking sheets with the melted butter, then dust them with flour. Spoon the batter onto the baking sheets using 2½ tsp. of batter per cookie. Stagger the rows and leave 1½" to 2" between each cookie. Prepare one cookie sheet at a time, keeping the remaining batter in the refrigerator.

3. Bake the cookies for seven to eight minutes, or until they are just beginning to brown around the edges, but are still pale in the center. Slide the cookies onto a wire rack to cool. They should keep for up to three days in an air-tight container.

You can tell by the enthusiasm in his voice and the spark in his eyes that Jason Dascoli, the executive chef at Jax Fish House, is passionate about his work. "Fish is definitely, by far, what I love to cook," he states. He can tell you the season for every type of fish you have ever heard of, and how to cook it.

His infatuation began in the first years of his life, living on the beach along the shore of Long Island, New York. He and his family moved to Boulder when he was 13, but he returned to the East Coast to attend culinary school. "I went to a small, hands-on type of school, the Southeast Culinary Institute in St. Augustine, Florida."

While in school, he moonlit at a large resort in St. Augustine and cooked at a fish house on the beach. Part of his job at the fish house was to go down to the docks and pick the fish that would be served that evening.

After graduating, Dascoli returned to Boulder, where he worked for a caterer and for the Flagstaff House. When Jax opened he applied for a job and, as he says, "persisted and persisted until I got an interview."

Dave Query, the owner of Jax, seems to have a sixth sense for choosing talented chefs. He hired Dascoli to handle the lunch crowd. When Jax stopped serving lunch, Query offered him the position of executive chef.

"This is my first big gig," says Dascoli. "As anyone can imagine, being down here on the Pearl Street Mall, especially working for Jax, is like a dream come true. When I wake up, I don't say 'Ugh, I've got to go to work,' I really enjoy what I do."

Dascoli describes the personnel at Jax as very solid. The house specials are developed by the entire cooking staff and each line cook has certain days when (s)he prepares the specials. Dascoli believes that this helps keep them not just interested, but enthusiastic. The wait staff is also very knowledgeable when it comes to

Jax Fish House

Jason Dascoli,
Executive Chef

928 Pearl Street,
Boulder
444-1811

fish and seafood. "They can go to the table and describe the featured fish or seafood and suggest wines to go with it."

Dascoli offers the following fish and seafood cooking tips: keep shellfish on ice, covered with a damp cloth; do not use mussels and clams that have no reaction when you tap them or that are wide open before cooking them. Dascoli uses scissors to shell shrimp. "Cut them along the top, forcing the shrimp straight. You can loosen the shell and get the vein at the same time."

Ultimately, Dascoli would like to own his own restaurant, but he says he has a lot to accomplish at Jax first. He would like to continue to be involved with Dave Query. "Not only is he the best chef I have ever worked for, but he is superior in the business world. He has a lot of good connections—a lot of his people have done good things and have really gone places."

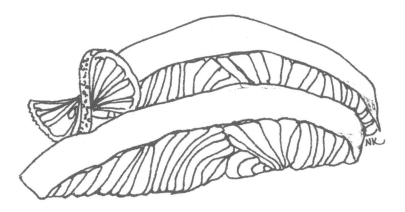

Conch Chowder

Serves: Six

This chowder is a meal in itself. Just serve it with crusty, warm sourdough bread. If conch meat is unavailable, substitute clams, shrimp or oysters. Dascoli adds, "Alligator meat would be killer!" (Sorry folks, I haven't a clue where to buy alligator.)

1. In a large saucepan or stock pot heat the olive oil over medium heat. Add the red and green bell peppers, onions, jalapeños, celery and potatoes. Cook, stirring often, until the onion and peppers are soft.

2. Stir in the garlic and continue cooking for about two more minutes. Stir in the chopped tomato, thyme, bay leaves oregano and cayenne. Cook for five minutes, then add the tomato juice. Raise the heat and reduce the liquid to about ¾ cup, stirring occasionally. Add the clam juice and conch meat, and simmer, partially covered, for 30 minutes. Add salt and pepper to taste.

*TIPS
—If you can find sweet white onions such as Vidalia, Maui or Walla Walla, use those.
—Conch is a shell fish native to the waters of Florida and the Caribbean. Their beautiful shells are often seen in souvenir shops. It's also the shell that is blown like a horn to signal the start of a luau. Conch are in season in summer. They can be found in Asian markets and other specialty groceries. They are also available frozen or canned.

¼ cup olive oil
2 cups chopped red bell pepper
1 cup chopped green bell pepper
1½ cups white onions*
2 jalapeños, stems removed, seeded and sliced into thin rings*
1 cup chopped celery
2 cups chopped Idaho potatoes, scrubbed but not peeled
¼ cup finely chopped garlic
½ cup chopped tomatoes
2 sprigs fresh thyme
2 bay leaves
1 Tbl. dry oregano
½ tsp. cayenne pepper
1 ½ cups tomato juice
3 cups bottled clam juice or fish stock
1 ½ lbs. conch meat, pounded to tenderize and minced
salt and pepper to taste

Jax Tuna Sashimi

Serves: Two as an appetizer

"I usually serve this only to V.I.P.'s and the people who know about it and love it," admits Dascoli. "They rave about this creamy potato and tuna dish."

2 small red potatoes
5 oz. Ahi tuna
Olive oil
salt and pepper
soy-honey sauce (recipe
      follows)
2 oz. pickled ginger, formed
      into a rosette*
1 oz. wasabi powder mixed
      with fresh lime juice to
      form a paste*
sweet soy sauce (optional)*

1. Steam or boil the potatoes for 15 to 20 minutes, until they are tender but still a little firm.

2. Lightly brush the tuna with oil and season it with salt and pepper. Grill the tuna to your liking, preferably rare.

3. To serve, thinly slice the tuna and the potatoes and alternate them on a platter to make a ring. In the center of the ring pour the soy-honey sauce. Place the pickled ginger rosette in the middle. Put a dollop of the wasabi on the side of the platter. If you desire, squirt sweet soy sauce decoratively around the platter.

1 cup soy sauce
¼ cup honey
1 tsp. mustard seed
2 Tbl. fresh lemon juice
1 Tbl. minced green onions
½ tsp. crushed red pepper

For the soy-honey sauce:
Place the soy sauce and honey in a small sauce pan. Bring it to a boil, then lower the heat to low and simmer for five minutes. Remove the pan from the heat and add the remaining ingredients. Blend well. Refrigerate for 30 minutes or more (this can be made up to a day ahead).

*TIPS
—To make a pickled ginger rosette: Gently wind the strips of ginger around and around, holding the bottom tighter than the top.
—Pickled ginger, wasabi and sweet soy sauce can all be found in Asian markets and some groceries.

Barbecued Salmon with Corn Pudding

Says Dascoli, "This dish is easy and fast but has the flare of the restaurant's best dishes. It's great in winter and early spring. Serve it with steamed Swiss chard and Corn Pudding (recipe follows).

1. Preheat the grill to medium-high and brush it with olive oil. Grill one side of the salmon for four minutes, then turn it.

2. Spread barbecue sauce on the cooked side and finish grilling. Place the fish on warm plates and serve with Swiss chard that has been steamed and tossed with butter and black pepper and corn pudding.

olive oil
4 (6-8 oz.) salmon fillets or
    steaks
salt and pepper
barbecue sauce (your favorite
    or try Don's Favorite BBQ
    sauce (page 78)

Corn Pudding

Serves: Four

1. Roast the corn in the oven or on the grill. When it's done and cool enough to handle, peel off the husks and cut off the kernels into a medium saucepan.

2. Add the milk to the corn and bring it to a boil. Stirring constantly, slowly whisk the corn meal into the milk and corn mixture. Cook over medium heat for five minutes, or until pudding has thickened. Season with salt and pepper to taste.

4 cups milk
1 ear fresh corn with husk
        in tact
½ cup corn meal
salt and pepper

John's Restaurant

John Bizzarro, Chef/Owner

2328 Pearl Street,
Boulder
444-5232

*W*hen John and Nancy Bizzarro opened John's in 1975, little did they know that America was on the brink of a culinary renaissance. The Bizzarros introduced Boulder to many of the lesser-known regional specialties of France, Spain and Italy that are now so popular, such as gnocchi, risotto and polenta. "Finding the essential ingredients in the '70s was a challenge," John recalls. "We grew a yard full of basil for our pestos. Fresh herbs were nonexistent in the market. A good variety of fresh fish was difficult to obtain as well."

About the same time the Bizzarros opened John's, Alice Waters founded Chez Panisse in Berkeley, where she created a new kind of Mediterranean cuisine with a fresh California approach. "We enthusiastically incorporated these taste sensations into our own dishes and menus," recounts John. Next came Creole and Cajun cooking and Bizzarro included those flavors as well.

"In 1984, a customer took me to Denver's first Vietnamese restaurant, the T-Wa Inn," says John. "Vietnamese cooking was a revelation to me and I began creating dishes that incorporated these hot-sweet-minty flavors with chile and garlic." Thai food followed quickly with spicy coconut curries and he began to do East-meets-West dishes. "Looking around Boulder today," says John, "I can't think of a culinary tradition that hasn't found its way to town."

John's is located in a charming, old clapboard cottage with a cozy dining area divided into several small sections, reminiscent of a rural French cafe, with its low-beamed ceilings and lace curtains. "Our concept was to create a small, country-style, family-owned restaurant with the proprietor-chef at the stove, similar to many we discovered during our travels in Europe and Mexico," Bizzarro says.

They opened John's with the backing and encouragement of David and Virginia Stainton who felt that a small, fine-dining restaurant was needed in Boulder. There is still fine dining to be had at John's today. John believes there is no end to learning in the kitchen, but that you don't need a restaurant to have fun and be creative. "These are exciting times for anyone who loves to cook, whether you're five or 85 years old. Creating and sharing is the name of the game called 'cooking.'"

Nancy's Carambola Salad

Serves: Four

John's wife Nancy grew up near a carambola grove in southern Florida. This salad is one of her favorites.

1. Arrange the baby red oak leaf lettuce around the edges of four salad plates.

2. Place the carambola, avocado, frisée, cucumber and onion in a large bowl.

3. In a small bowl, mash the peppercorns and blend with the olive oil. Add this mixture to the large bowl of fruit and vegetables and toss. Add salt to taste. Add the vinegar and toss just enough to distribute evenly.

4. Divide the salad among the plates, placing it in the middle of the oak leaf lettuce and serve.

12 baby red oak lettuce leaves
2 ripe carambolas, sliced into ¼" stars*
2 ripe avocados, cut into ½" cubes
2 cups (apx.) frisée leaves
½ cucumber (English cucumber if available), sliced into ¼" rounds
¼ red onion, sliced thinly
12 green peppercorns from a jar (not dried)
2 Tbl. olive oil
salt
2 Tbl. balsamic vinegar

*TIPS
—Carambola is a tropical fruit that grows in the Caribbean, Hawaii, Latin America and parts of Southeast Asia. It looks like a star when cut crosswise and is often called "star fruit." When ripe, it is very juicy and fragrant, and has a sweet taste with a refreshing hint of tart. Carambolas are in season from the end of summer to mid-winter. Buy the most yellow ones and keep them refrigerated. Carambolas also make a very attractive garnish.

Roasted Red Peppers with Chévre and Mozzarella

4 red bell peppers, roasted and
   skinned (see Before
   Beginning)
4 oz. chévre (goat cheese)
2 oz. fresh buffalo mozzarella,*
   sliced very thinly
salt and pepper
2 tomatoes, blanched, peeled
   and seeded (see Before
   Beginning)
2 Tbl. olive oil
1 small garlic clove, chopped
2 tsp. balsamic vinegar
fresh basil leaves cut into tiny
   strips

Serves: Four as an appetizer

1. Preheat the oven to 350°. Make a slit lengthwise in each of the roasted peppers. Drain off any juice and remove the seeds, being careful not to tear the pepper.

2. Divide the goat cheese and mozzarella into four equal parts and stuff each pepper. Sprinkle with salt and pepper. Place on an oiled baking sheet and bake for approximately eight minutes, or until the cheese is melted.

3. While the peppers are baking, place the tomatoes, olive oil, garlic and vinegar in a blender and process until smooth. Add salt to taste.

4. To assemble, spoon the tomato vinaigrette onto each of four salad plates. Place a stuffed pepper on the vinaigrette and garnish with basil strips.

*TIPS
—Buffalo mozzarella is a fresh mozzarella, often made with a combination of cow and water buffalo milk. Fresh mozzarellas are softer and sweeter than other mozzarellas. Buffalo mozzarella can be found packed in water in many groceries. If buffalo mozzarella is unavailable, you may substitute fresh cow's milk mozzarella.

Chile Crusted Breast of Duck with Cranberry Orange Salsa

Serves: Two for dinner or Four for a light supper

If you don't want to carve the duck yourself, ask the butcher to remove the breasts for you, but be sure to get the rest of the duck. Freeze the legs and thighs for another meal. The rest of the duck and the bones can be used to make stock. Everything but the cooking of the duck can be done in advance.

1 cup cranberries* (fresh or frozen)
zest of 1 orange
juice of 1 orange
1 cup sugar
1 cup balsamic vinegar
¼ cup flour
¼ cup ground mild red chile (not chili powder)
1 tsp. salt
1 tsp. pepper
1 tsp. thyme
1 tsp. garlic powder
2 whole duck breasts
olive oil
1 head radicchio,* shredded

1. To make the salsa, combine the cranberries, orange zest and juice in a heavy saucepan. Cook over medium heat until the cranberries pop open; about 15 minutes. Add ½ cup of the sugar and cook, stirring, until the sugar has dissolved. Cool in the pan (don't wash the pan yet). Pour into a strainer, reserving the juice for the sauce. Refrigerate the salsa until ready to use.

2. For the sauce, use the same saucepan used to make the salsa. Combine the balsamic vinegar and the other ½ cup of sugar. Stir over the heat until the sugar has dissolved. Bring to a boil and cook until the mixture has reduced to ½ to ¾ cup. Add the reserved juice from the cranberry salsa. The sauce should be the consistency of thick olive oil and should not run when spooned onto a flat plate. If it is too thin, boil it a little longer. Cool and set aside. Refrigerate if not using within a few hours.

3. For the duck, place the flour, chile, salt, pepper, thyme and garlic powder in a plastic bag and shake to mix thoroughly. Place the duck breasts in the bag and shake to coat them evenly with the flour mixture.

4. Coat a heavy skillet with olive oil. Heat on high until the oil is very hot. Add the duck breasts and cook for four or five minutes on each side, until done to your taste.*

5. To serve, warm the salsa and the sauce. Arrange the radicchio on warm plates. Skin the duck and thinly slice. Arrange the slices atop the radicchio. Drizzle about one tablespoon of sauce over the duck. Garnish with a spoonful of cranberry salsa. Pass the extra sauce and salsa.

TIPS
—Fresh cranberries are available from about Halloween through December. Any that are discolored or shriveled should be discarded. Cranberries are very high in vitamin C and can be frozen for up to a year.
—Radicchio is a red-leafed Italian lettuce available most of the year. Buy heads that show no signs of browning. They can be stored in the refrigerator for up to four days.
—The skin can be removed from the duck breast before cooking if desired.

Peaches in Chianti

4 fresh, ripe peaches, skinned, pitted and halved (see Before Beginning)
2 cups Chianti
½ cup Amaretto liqueur
6 oz. mascarpone cheese
¼ cup whipping cream
⅓ cup whole blanched almonds, toasted

Serves: Four to Eight, depending on the number of peach halves you serve each person.

1. Place the peaches in a glass bowl with the Chianti and ¼ cup of the Amaretto. Cover with plastic wrap and marinate for a day or two in the refrigerator.

2. Mix the mascarpone, whipping cream and the remaining ¼ cup of Amaretto.

3. When ready to serve, drain the peaches and place one or two peach halves in a chilled bowl. Spoon mascarpone cream over the peaches and garnish with the almonds.

*I*n 1976, John Lehndorff was selling food from a sandwich cart on Pearl Street. Now, Lehndorff is the award-winning food editor of Boulder's *Daily Camera*. How did he get from peddling sandwiches to overseeing the food scene in Boulder?

Lehndorff can't remember a time when he wasn't interested in food. "When I was a kid, I worked for a caterer in the summers putting on clam bakes." After the sandwich cart, Lehndorff worked for a number of local restaurants. At the same time, he was writing freelance and being featured in Front Range magazines and newspapers such as the *Colorado Daily* and *Boulder Magazine*. The *Camera* hired him in 1985.

Since starting at the *Camera*, Lehndorff has developed a broad following, and his column, "Nibbles," is nationally syndicated. "Being food editor is a minimum amount of fun and lots of story editing, meetings and dealing with press releases. What I really enjoy is doing the column," he says. In "Nibbles," Lehndorff shares his life with readers. As a result, he gets mail from all over the country, often asking about his son, Hans, his wife, Betsy, and even what he's planning to grow in his garden in the summer. "It's interesting being a public person; everyone knows what I eat, what foods I crave and stories about my family."

Lehndorff has won awards for food writing and editing, and has written for such newspapers as *The Washington Post* and *The Chicago Tribune*. He has even hosted a weekly radio show. Lehndorff also considers himself a veteran food judge, officiating at numerous pie contests, chocolate competitions and chili cookoffs. Like many of the chefs and restaurant owners in Boulder County, Lehndorff has given much time toward charitable causes. In addition to working for Boulder County Community Food Shares, Lehndorff was the

John Lehndorff

Food Editor, Daily Camera / Executive Director, American Pie Council

PO Box 591,
Boulder, CO 80306
473-1335

founder of "A Taste of the Nation" in Boulder, an annual event in which local chefs cook to raise money for hunger relief. Another group to which Lehndorff gives his time is the American Pie Council.

Lehndorff refers to the Pie Council as his other life. He says, tongue not entirely in cheek, "If more people ate pie, this would be a better world." The Pie Council has been in existence since 1981, but mostly just to celebrate National Pie Day, January 23. Lehndorff is working hard to make it into a real association, especially since the National Pie Championships moved from Nevada to Boulder in 1997. He has developed a membership brochure and is working on a quarterly newsletter called *Pie Times*. Even the World Wide Web may soon have pies on its menu. Lehndorff is hoping to garner local sponsorship and support for the Pie Council. His goal is to make Boulder the "pie capital" of the nation.

It is not surprising that one of Lehndorff's recipes is a pie—a fabulous peach pie with a crumb and nut topping. He also shares a favorite family recipe for stuffing.

John Lehndorff's Favorite Colorado Peach Pie

Serves: Six to Eight

"A year before our son was born, the craggy old peach trees in our backyard burst forth with a bevy of blossoms unlike any I had ever seen. As the season progressed, the limbs creaked from the weight of hundreds of fine Colorado peaches. In autumn, I helped (my wife) Betsy harvest the huge fruits as an early snow fell. We peeled and sliced them, and froze them for later use.

"After we brought our newborn son home from the hospital, I decided to make a pie to celebrate the event using those peaches. I've made a lot of pies in my life but few tasted so sweet, as I shared it with my wife and two sisters. I even put a dab in Hans' mouth. He has loved pie ever since. The trees have not yielded such a big harvest again." Lehndorff recommends serving this pie for breakfast, lunch, dinner or dessert.

2-3 lbs. Colorado peaches, peeled and thickly sliced (about 8 or 9 peaches or 6 cups sliced)* (see Before Beginning)

2-4 Tbl. lemon juice, more or less, depending on the sweetness of the peaches*

¾-1 cup sugar, more or less, depending on the sweetness of the peaches*

1 Tbl. flour

2 Tbl. quick-cooking pearl tapioca, pulverized to a powder in blender

pie shell and lattice strips (recipe follows)

3 Tbl. butter

water or eggwhites, slightly beaten

milk

Crumb topping (recipe follows)

sugar

1. Preheat the oven to 450°. In a large bowl, mix the peaches with the lemon juice, sugar, flour and tapioca. If the mixture seems too wet and runny, add a little more flour to it. Densely pack the peach mixture into the pie shell, mounding the mixture in the middle, allowing few air pockets or spaces. Dot with the butter.

2. Lay the dough strips across the peaches vertically and then horizontally to form a lattice (see pie crust recipe). Moisten the ends of the strips with water or egg whites to "glue" them to the edge of the crust. Brush the lattice strips lightly with milk. This helps them brown. Pack the crumb mixture (recipe follows) between the lattice strips, but do not cover the strips. Sprinkle the top of the pie with sugar.

3. Bake the pie for 15 minutes on a lower or middle rack in the oven. Turn the heat down to 400° and bake for another 40 minutes, or until the middle of the pie is bubbly and the crumb topping is browned. If the top is browning too quickly, cover it with a double layer of foil, then remove the foil for the last 15 minutes of baking.

4. Cool the pie on a rack for at least 20 minutes before slicing. Serve with whipped cream or vanilla ice cream.

*TIPS
—Lehndorff suggests tossing the peaches with a little fresh lemon juice and a little sugar so they don't turn brown before using them. At this point, the peaches can be frozen for up to six months. Thaw them before using. You can freeze the dough and even the whole unbaked pie for up to six months.

3 cups flour, plus additional as needed
1½ tsp. salt
1 Tbl. sugar
1 cup shortening, chilled
⅓ cup butter, chilled
1 egg, slightly beaten
5 Tbl. ice-cold water, plus additional as needed
1 Tbl. lemon juice
egg wash (1 egg beaten with 1 tsp. of milk)

For John Lehndorff's pie crust:
1. Mix the flour, salt and sugar in a large bowl. With a chilled fork, cut the shortening and butter into the flour mixture.

2. Mix the egg, water and the lemon juice and add the mixture to the flour. Blend again with a chilled fork. If the dough is too wet and sticky, add more flour. If it is too dry, add more water. Do not over mix the dough or it will be tough. It should have an easy-to-handle, smooth consistency.

3. Divide the dough in half and form it into even disks or flattened rounds. Wrap the dough in plastic and refrigerate for 15 minutes. Thinly roll out half the dough on a floured board or cloth about 12" wide. Invert the dough into a 9" pie pan. The dough should hang over the edge of the pie pan by 1". Trim and attractively crimp the edges of the dough, and brush the edges with the egg wash.

4. Roll out the remaining dough and cut it into ¼" strips (these are used for the lattice top). If you have a pastry wheel or pastry cutter with scalloped edges, use it to cut the strips; it gives them an attractive edge.

For the crumb topping:
Combine the topping ingredients and mix well.

Variations:
In the topping, replace the walnuts with pine nuts.
In the filling, replace ½ cup of peaches with ½ cup of dried blueberries or sour Colorado cherries.
In the crust, replace ½ cup of flour with ½ cup of ground almonds.

¼ cup chopped walnuts
¼ cup ground, toasted almonds
¼ cup flour
½ cup brown sugar
6 Tbl. butter
1 Tbl. vanilla
⅛ tsp. freshly ground nutmeg
pinch of cinnamon
pinch of ginger
pinch of salt

Thanksgiving Potato-Sausage Stuffing

Makes: enough stuffing for a large turkey with extra on the side

The stuffing needs to be prepared a day in advance.

Lehndorff says, "It's not that I don't like a good bread stuffing. I do, and I'm happy to eat it at the big feast, but without potato-sausage stuffing, it would not be Thanksgiving for me. I am not a traditionalist in most culinary matters, but every year I make the stuffing in exactly the same way on the night before the feast.

"There has never been a recipe that I know of for this wonderful stuffing. The formula encoded in my memory guides me as I stand before the stove, as it did for my mother, Rose, and her mother, Vincenza. My mother tells me that the recipe came from a French family, that lived down the hall from her Sicilian family. The French family, too, had adopted and adapted it in the great, all-American, culture-fusing fashion.

"Now I'm teaching my son Hans. He already has one year of stuffing-making experience. He stood on a step ladder last year and helped stir the potatoes. On some proud Thanksgiving eve, Hans will take over the stuffing duties, which include peeling lots of potatoes.

"To make the stuffing, I buy a variety of potatoes: some white, some red, some yellow, some bakers, some boilers. Five pounds is a nice round number. You can never make too many mashed potatoes. I know I'll eat a half-pound just getting the spicing right. I peel the potatoes while listening to the traditional album, *Europe '72* by the Grateful Dead. I then wash, drain and cut the potatoes into big chunks and cover them with cold water in the large, heirloom aluminum pan that my grandmother once used. The potatoes are boiled until sort of tender, but not at all mushy.

"While the spuds cook, I get out my immense, black, cast iron frying pan. I crumble chunks of freshly made sweet and hot Italian sausage into the pan, along with some ground pork (the sausage is in memory of my grandfather, Michael Mazzola, a Sicilian grocer in Willamantic, Connecticut, who made memorable sausage in the back of his store). The meat gets fried just until the pink is barely gone (but not until it is completely cooked; it finishes cooking inside the turkey). Then all of the fat gets drained off.

"The magic moment occurs when the sausage is added to the very lumpy mashers. As I taste it, and then taste it again to assure its authenticity and adjust the spices, I once again realize why I always make twice as much as I could possibly serve. Potatoes and sausage together are absolutely, addictively delicious. The mixture develops additional flavor nuances as it ages over several days, or is happily discovered in the freezer on a tired, January weekday night.

"The next morning, in the dark, I will force the stuffing into the nooks and crannies of the deceased bird, a replacement for its heart and soul. It's not a pretty sight, but it's an honest one in this age when our meat is processed far from our squeamish sight. I thank the turkey as I close the oven and wait to hear Arlo Guthrie's epic "Alice's Restaurant" on the radio—another Thanksgiving tradition.

"The excess stuffing gets baked and served in a dish, but it tastes different from that which emerges moistly glistening with gobbler fat and roast turkey flavor. I sometimes add some onions or garlic, though my mother never would because, she said, 'Your father won't eat it.' Still, I never deviate too far from the proscribed taste. This is not the day for innovation."

5 lbs. potatoes (white, yellow, red, bakers, boilers, etc.), peeled and coarsely chopped
cold water
1¾ lbs. sweet Italian sausage
1¾ lbs. hot Italian sausage
¾ lb. ground pork
1 cup chopped onion
2 garlic cloves, minced
1 stick butter, or more to taste
salt and pepper
1 tsp. poultry seasoning, or more depending on taste
1 Tbl. minced fresh sage, or more depending on taste

1. Place the potatoes in a large saucepan or stockpot filled with enough cold water to cover the potatoes. Bring the potatoes to boil over high heat, and boil until just tender.

2. While the potatoes are cooking, crumble the sausage and pork into a large, heavy skillet. Add the onion and cook over medium heat, stirring often. When the pink color of the meat is nearly gone, add the garlic and stir well. When the pink color is just barely gone, remove the mixture from the heat and pour off the fat.

3. When the potatoes are done, drain them (reserve the potato water for making soups later). Immediately return the potatoes to the pot in which they cooked and add the butter. Stir, but do not mash, the potatoes until the butter has melted. Add salt and pepper to taste, then add the poultry seasoning and sage.

4. Add the sausage mixture to the potatoes and stir until well combined. Taste for seasoning and adjust the salt, pepper, poultry seasoning and sage as needed. Refrigerate overnight. Bring to room temperature before stuffing the turkey. Bake the leftover stuffing in an oiled baking dish covered with foil at 325° until well heated.

"*T*he best Mexican food I've eaten has always been in a dump," states Roger Berardi, owner of Juanita's. Berardi had been toying with the idea of doing a Mexican restaurant in Boulder for about three or four years before Juanita's became a reality. "I had always talked about doing a 'divey' Mexican restaurant, but we could never find the right location," he says.

Berardi more or less grew up in the restaurant business. His family moved to Boulder County in 1951 when Berardi was a toddler. "My dad got started in the restaurant business because he knew how to make spaghetti," says Berardi. "He would cook it for the high school and do big dinners for people. Everybody said he should be in the restaurant business, so in 1961 he opened a restaurant in Louisville called the Wagon Wheel."

When Berardi finally found a location for his Mexican restaurant on Pearl Street, the fun started. "It was kind of a lark. I painted the place red and did lots of crazy things."

And it works. The floors are wood, a huge mural takes up one wall, Mexican rugs and blankets hang on the other walls and are draped over the booths in the main room. In back is the bar, a pool table and many televisions spouting the game of the hour.

But what about the food? "We had not had that much experience with Mexican food," admits Berardi. "So we traveled around finding items that we liked. The green chile is unique to Colorado. I learned to make it when I was a kid from one of the cooks at my Dad's restaurant."

What Berardi especially likes are really greasy tacos cooked in lard, but he realizes that they would not go over in health-conscious Boulder. Instead, the bill of fare ranges from fajitas and traditional burritos and tacos to an honest and delicious posole (pork and hominy stew) and a savory braised halibut.

Juanita's Mexican Food

Roger Berardi, Owner

1043 Pearl Street
Boulder
449-5273

One of Berardi's goals is to be "a facilitator for young people." Among his partners are a former bartender and a former wait person. "They now have a piece of the action." He is impressed with the new generation of young people bringing about this "new wave" of food and is eager to encourage them.

Braised Halibut Vera Cruz

Serves: Four

This is an easy, do-ahead dish that works with many different kinds of fish. Use your imagination!

¼ cup minced onion
1 jalapeño pepper, seeded and minced (see Before Beginning)
2 tsp. minced garlic
½ tsp. lemon zest
1½ Tbl. capers
¾ cup sliced green olives* plus whole olives for garnish
¼ tsp. black pepper
2 Tbl. butter
4-6 (8 oz.) portions halibut or sea bass
1 cinnamon stick
¼ cup water
slices of lemon for garnish

1. Combine the onion, jalapeño, garlic, lemon zest, capers, olives and pepper in a small bowl. Cover and place in the refrigerator until ready to use.

2. In a skillet large enough to fit the fish, melt the butter over high heat until bubbling. Add the fish and cook for one minute on each side. Lower the heat and add the cinnamon stick and water. Cover the pan and cook for a few more minutes until the fish is done to your liking.

3. To serve, place the fish on warm plates with the onion-caper mixture on part of the tops and sides of the fish. Garnish with a lemon slice and a couple of whole olives.

*TIPS
—Use pitted green olives if possible to save time. Do not use the Spanish type of olives stuffed with pimento.

Caldo de Chipotle

Serves: Four

This is a surprisingly delightful and spicy soup.

1. In a large saucepan heat the butter until it is melted and bubbling. Add the onions and cook over medium heat for 10 minutes. Add the garlic and continue cooking until onions are soft, taking care not to brown the garlic. Add the thyme, marjoram, basil, oregano, chile caribe, chile powder and salt. Cook over low heat, stirring occasionally. Add the flour and stir over low heat until smooth. Add the sherry and stir constantly over low heat until blended well. Add the bay leaf.

2. Combine the milk, cream and chipotles. Stirring constantly, add this mixture to the onion mixture. Raise the heat to medium-high. Add the water and continue stirring until well blended. Bring the mixture to a boil, then lower the heat and simmer for 20 minutes. Serve in heated soup bowls. Garnish with a sprig of cilantro.

*TIPS
—Chile caribe is best known as the red chile flakes used as a pizza topping. They are medium hot.
—New Mexican chile powder is found in the Mexican aisle of most groceries. It is different than chili powder found in the spice aisle. It is mild to medium-hot.
—Chipotles are smoked jalapeños. They add a deep, smoky flavor and are hot to very hot. Canned chipotles are available in the Mexican food aisle of most groceries. If you cannot find canned, use one whole dried chipotle soaked in warm water for 30 minutes. Remove the stem and seed, and chop it before adding it to the caldo.

¼ cup butter
1 cup chopped onions
¼ cup minced garlic
1 tsp. thyme
1 tsp. marjoram
1 tsp. basil
1 tsp. oregano
1 Tbl. chile caribe (red chile flakes)*
1½ tsp. New Mexican chile powder*
2 tsp. salt
½ cup flour
¼ cup sherry
1 bay leaf
1½ cups milk
¼ cup heavy cream
½ can chipotle peppers*, or less to taste
2 cups water
cilantro sprigs to garnish

Juanita's Flan

Serves: Six

Juanita's famous flan is a favorite at both the Boulder and Denver restaurants.

½ cup sugar
½ cup water
1 quart milk
½ cup sugar
4 eggs
4 egg whites
1½ tsp. vanilla
berries or other fruit to garnish

1. Preheat the oven to 375°. Combine the sugar and water in a small saucepan and bring to a boil. Stirring occasionally, reduce the mixture to the consistency of a thick syrup.

2. Coat the bottom of six ramekins or individual soufflé dishes with the syrup. Place the ramekins in a baking dish or a pan large enough to fit all of them.

3. In a medium saucepan, bring the milk and sugar to a boil, then reduce the heat and simmer for 15 minutes. Place a kettle of water over high heat for a water bath.

4. Combine the eggs, egg whites and vanilla in a mixing bowl and beat for one minute (If you have a choice of beaters, use the wire whisk attachment.). Slowly add the hot milk mixture to the eggs, beating constantly. Pour this mixture over the syrup in the bottom of the ramekins.

5. Place the ramekins in the baking dish and pour enough hot water around the dishes to come with 1" to 2" of the tops. Be careful not to get any water in the custard. Cover the baking pan with foil and bake for about 25 minutes. The flan should be just firm when done.

6. Cool and then chill before serving. To serve, unmold the flan upside down on a dessert plate.Garnish with berries or other fruit.

KT's Barbecue

Tricia and Kirk Jamison, Co-Owners

7464 Arapahoe Road,
Boulder
786-7608

2675 13th Street,
Boulder
442-3717

*T*ricia and Kirk Jamison are proof that preparation, planning, research and hard work can pay off. In fewer than three-and-a-half years they have gone from living out of their truck, to owning two restaurants in Boulder County.

The Jamisons met at Seattle University where Tricia was a technical writing major and Kirk was studying hotel and restaurant management. They often talked about their post-graduation plans and discovered that they were on the same wavelength; they both wanted to open a small restaurant. After graduating and getting married, they began to work on a business plan. Says Tricia, "We did significant market research to determine what to cook and where to go. There was a barbecue restaurant in Seattle that was a mom and pop place, just like what we wanted. It was in an old, converted gas station and always had a line out the door." That restaurant lead them to choose barbecue.

Once they had decided on the type of restaurant, they began to research where they would relocate. They discovered that Boulder had many little areas of light industry where there were few, if any, restaurants. They looked in Gunbarrel and several other locations with no luck. "Then one day we were driving down Arapahoe Road and saw this quaint little house. It was perfect! The zoning was right and the numbers were right. It was like angels were looking over our shoulders."

In the meantime, they were madly working on recipes. "Kirk went to Memphis and ate nothing but barbecue for a solid week," grins Tricia. He visited large and small restaurants, asking people what their favorite type of barbecue was and why. Tricia remembers, "He came back with this vinegar-based recipe that I couldn't stand. I grew up eating the sweeter type of sauce. So I said, 'I'll come up with my own sauce.'" When KT's opened they served two different sauces. Many of their customers complained that their sauces were not hot enough. "Almost as a joke, we made the hottest sauce we could think up. The funny thing is, they loved it." This sauce was dubbed "Double Diamond Sauce."

When the Jamisons first moved to Boulder, they lived out of their truck until they found a place in Lafayette. By the time they opened, they had no money left for advertising and had to depend on word of mouth for six months. By virtue of good food and good fortune, KT's caught on. They moved from the tiny little house on Arapahoe Road to a much larger location at the corner of Arapahoe Road and 75th Street. They then opened a second KT's on 13th street, in the back of the shopette that houses Boulder Wine Merchant and Moe's Bagels.

KT's offers Boulderites true barbecue: mouth-watering pork, Texas beef brisket, smoked chicken, spicy pork and beef sausages and ribs. The Killer Beans are as good as their name and the cole slaw is a refreshing, tasty take on the old standard.

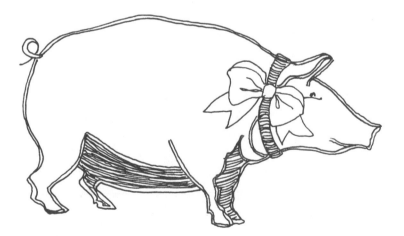

KT's Famous Cole Slaw

Serves: Four to Six

"This coleslaw is great all by itself, but is dynamite served atop a barbecued pork sandwich," says Tricia.

1. In a large bowl, combine the cabbage, onion and carrot, and toss.

2. In a small saucepan, combine the brown sugar and vinegar. Stir over medium heat until the sugar dissolves. Cool slightly. Remove the pan from the heat and cool slightly. Add the mustard, cayenne and black peppers, and mayonnaise. Mix thoroughly.

3. Pour the dressing over the cabbage mixture and toss. If you like a crunchy cole slaw, serve immediately. If you like a softer slaw, let it stand for one hour before serving.

TIPS
—To prepare the cabbage, first cut it in half. Remove the core and the outer leaves. Trim away the tough ribs. Shred the cabbage with a sharp knife.

1 small head of cabbage,
    shredded*
½ small onion, chopped
1 carrot, peeled and grated
¼ cup brown sugar
2 tsp. cider vinegar
2 Tbl. yellow mustard
¼ tsp. cayenne pepper
1 tsp. black pepper
1 cup mayonnaise

Easy Enchiladas

Serves: Four to Six

These are a Jamison family favorite. You can freeze the enchiladas as well as the leftovers (if there are any). Tricia serves the enchiladas with Spanish rice and refried beans.

2-3 Tbl. olive oil
2 medium onions, chopped
2 lbs. KT's smoked beef brisket, shredded*
3 cups grated cheddar cheese
1 (4½ oz.) can diced green chilies
10-12 flour tortillas
1 (10 oz.) can enchilada sauce
1 head romaine lettuce, shredded
1 bunch cilantro, chopped
2-3 fresh tomatoes, chopped

1. Heat the olive oil and sauté the onions in it until soft.

2. Preheat the oven to 350°. Evenly spread an equal amount of the brisket, onions, 2¼ cups of the cheese and the chilies over each tortilla. Roll up the tortillas and place them in a flat, oiled baking dish, seam-side down.

2. Pour enchilada sauce over the enchiladas and sprinkle them with the remaining ¾ cup of cheese. Loosely cover the pan with foil and bake for 40 to 50 minutes, until the enchiladas are hot and bubbling.

3. Serve the enchiladas on warm plates, garnished with lettuce, cilantro and tomatoes.

*TIPS
—Smoked beef brisket can be found at many BBQ restaurants.

Risotto with Mushrooms and Leeks

Serves: Four

This recipe may also be made in a pressure cooker.*

1. Heat the butter and oil in a medium skillet. Add the leeks and mushrooms and cook over medium heat until the leeks are soft. Add the rice. Cook, stirring, until the rice turns translucent.

2. Add the broth, ½ cup at a time, stirring often. Wait until one addition of broth is absorbed before adding another. When all of the liquid has been absorbed, the risotto should be done and have a creamy consistency with a very slight crunch (al dente).

3. Stir in the cheese. Add salt and pepper to taste. Serve immediately.

*TIPS
—If you have a pressure cooker you can cook the risotto much faster. To make it in the pressure cooker, melt the butter and oil in the cooker. Sauté the leeks in the butter and oil until soft, but not brown. Add the rice, stirring to coat it with the butter or oil. Stir in the mushrooms and then add the broth. Lock the lid in place and bring the cooker to high pressure. Maintain high pressure for 8½ minutes. Reduce the pressure with the quick-release method. Place the cooker under cold running water until it cools enough to be handled. Remove the lid and stir in the Parmesan. Add salt and pepper to taste. Serve immediately.

1 Tbl. butter
1 Tbl. olive oil
2 medium leeks, white part only, cleaned well and thinly sliced
½ lb. mushrooms, stems removed, caps thinly sliced
1½ cups Arborio rice
3½ cups vegetable or chicken broth
½ cup grated Parmesan cheese
salt and pepper

Munson Farms

Chris and Jennifer Munson

75th & Valmont,
Boulder
941-2026

*I*f you have lived in Boulder for any length of time, you have probably enjoyed Chris and Jennifer Munson's sweet corn, available from their stand at 75th and Valmont, at farmer's markets or in local restaurants.

Chris is the third generation of Munsons to work in the produce business in Boulder County. Jennifer, however, is a newcomer, both to the Munson family and to life on the farm. Jennifer grew up in Philadelphia and first came to Colorado to study marketing at the University of Colorado. She met Chris, a mechanical engineering major, during her final semester.

After graduation, Jennifer and Chris moved to San Francisco and worked there for almost two years. When Chris's father called and asked him to come back and run the family farm, Chris asked Jennifer to come with him. She had mixed feelings about making such a drastic lifestyle change. "But then he proposed," she says with a big smile on her face. "We decided that instead of me trying to get another job and Chris working the farm, we would run it together." Jennifer handles the business end and takes care of their son. "I take absolutely no credit for the vegetables and their fresh taste. That's all Chris. He is truly the work-horse, the one who knows what he's doing as far as the crops."

Jennifer and Chris have tripled the size of the farm in four years. Although Munson's is best known for their sweet corn, they grow many other vegetables including tomatoes, basil, squash and pumpkins. Jennifer shares a recipe from her collection as well as one each from her mother-in-law and sister-in-law.

Pumpkin and Coconut Cream Soup

Serves: Four

This delicious soup is from Chris's mother, Marcy. She recommends using pie pumpkin, as jack-o'-lantern pumpkin is too stringy. Serve the soup with French bread and a good Chardonnay.

1. Peel and seed the pumpkin and cut it into ½" pieces. Set aside. In a large sauce pan, heat the olive oil. Add the garlic and shallots and stir. Cook until almost soft, but not brown. Add the chiles or pepper flakes and shrimp paste. Stir over the heat for one minute.

2. Add the chicken broth and pumpkin. Bring to a boil, then turn down the heat so that the mixture is barely bubbling. Cover the pan and simmer for 15 minutes.

3. Stir in the coconut milk and simmer, covered, for another 10 minutes, or until the pumpkin is tender (up to this point, the soup may be prepared several hours before serving).

4. Heat the soup to the boiling point. Add the shrimp and cook over medium heat until the shrimp are done; about five minutes. Ladle the soup into four warm bowls and sprinkle a little minced basil on top.

1 small (apx. 2 lbs.) pie
    pumpkin*
2 Tbl. olive oil
1 large garlic clove, minced
4 shallots, finely chopped
2 small red chiles, minced
    (or ½ tsp. red pepper
    flakes)
½ tsp. shrimp paste*
3 cups chicken broth
1 (14 oz.) can coconut milk*
½ lb. medium shrimp, peeled
    and deveined
1 Tbl. minced fresh basil

*TIPS
—Fresh pumpkins are available in the fall and winter. In general, smaller pumpkins are more tender and have a better flavor. Some of the mild, sweet squashes could be substituted for pumpkin, if pumpkin is unavailable. Whole pumpkins keep well at room temperature for about a month or refrigerated for up to three months. Pumpkins are a good source of vitamin A.
—Shrimp paste and coconut milk can be found in Asian markets or in the Asian section of some groceries.

Joan Simeo-Munson's White Corn Soup with Poblano Chile Purée

Serves: Four to Six

1 large poblano chile
2½ cups + 1 Tbl. chicken (or vegetable) stock; plus more if needed
3 Tbl. butter
¾ cup chopped onion
5 cups Munson white corn kernels (about 5 medium ears)*
salt and pepper
4-6 dollops (apx. 1 Tbl. each) heavy cream
¼ cup chopped fresh cilantro

1. Roast and peel the chile (see Before Beginning). Remove the stem and seeds and coarsely chop. Purée the chile in a blender with one tablespoon of stock.

2. Melt the butter in a heavy, large saucepan over medium-low heat. Add the onion and sauté until tender; about 10 minutes. Add the corn and cook for two minutes longer. Add the 2½ cups of stock and bring to a boil. Reduce the heat and simmer until the corn is tender; about six minutes. Cool slightly and then purée the soup in batches. Return to saucepan and season with salt and pepper. Reheat the soup (if it is too thick, add more stock).

3. Ladle the soup into warm bowls. Place a dollop of the chile purée and a dollop of cream in each bowl and swirl decoratively. Sprinkle with cilantro.

*TIPS
—The chile purée can be made one day in advance. Keep it covered and refrigerated. Bring it to room temperature before using it.
—If white corn is unavailable, you can substitute other Munson sweet corn varieties.

Cucumber Vichyssoise

Serves: Ten

This soup tastes best if chilled overnight and if the freshest ingredients are used.

1. In a medium to large saucepan, simmer the potatoes in the stock for 20 minutes, or until tender. While the potatoes are cooking, sauté the leeks and onion in the butter until soft. When the potatoes are done, add the leeks, onions, and cucumber.

2. Purée the soup in batches in a blender or food processor. Return the purée to the saucepan and stir in the cream. Refrigerate until cold (ideally overnight). Season with salt and pepper to taste after the soup is cold. Serve cold, topped with fresh chives.

3 cups peeled, cubed potatoes
5 cups chicken (or vegetable) stock
3 cups sliced leeks
1 small onion, diced
2 Tbl. butter
1 large Munson cucumber, peeled, seeded and diced
1½ cups heavy cream
salt and pepper
chopped, fresh chives to garnish

Nancy's Restaurant

Arnie Schmollinger, Chef/Co-owner

825 Walnut Street,
Boulder
499-8402

*I*n 1972, Nancy Von Loon discovered a diner on The Hill that was willing to rent its six stools to her for three dollars a morning. She proceeded to introduce Boulderites to quiche, croissants and blintzes. Her restaurant caught on quickly and she soon needed a larger space. She chose a location on 14th Street (now Lucile's), which had housed a bakery. In 1977, she purchased the charming house on Walnut Street, where Nancy's is now located.

In 1979, a young man named Arnie Schmollinger arrived in Boulder and applied for a job at Nancy's. Schmollinger grew up in Connecticut surrounded by family from Poland, Bavaria, Italy and other middle and eastern European countries. He grew increasingly interested in preparing the wonderful variety of dishes he had taken for granted throughout his life. In his teens, he began to experiment and found that he really enjoyed working in the kitchen.

Schmollinger's initiation into the food industry took place in an Italian restaurant. "The owner was a rum runner and his wife ran a bordello," confides Schmollinger. "I witnessed gambling, bookies at work, even murders." Rapidly tiring of the situation, Schmollinger moved to Key West. He spent two years there working for a "great chef," who was one of the writers of the Time-Life *Foods of the World* cookbook series. Schmollinger spent his time there living in a tent. "My rent was only 90 dollars a month," he remembers. "I had no coat or long pants until I moved to Boulder." He soon became Von Loon's chef, and in 1987 he became her business partner.

Nancy's is best known for breakfast. In 1995, *Travel & Leisure* magazine selected it as one of the best places in the country for breakfast, recommending it for "eggs Benedict loyalists." In 1995 the *Daily Camera* reported, "About the only place to sample a 'proper' English scone in Boulder is at Nancy's." There are interesting and delicious lunch and dinner dishes as well. Two of the recipes Schmollinger submitted, the avocado grapefruit salad and the chicken breast Malanzani are original recipes from Nancy's. He completes the menu with a decadent chocolate-raspberry cake.

Avocado Grapefruit Salad with Tequila Green Chile Dressing

Serves: Six

This salad's refreshing flavors make it a delight, especially on a hot summer day.

1. In a heavy saucepan, combine the tequila, green chilies, cumin, salt, honey, water, coriander, orange and lime juices. Bring to a boil, then lower the heat to a simmer. Add the cornstarch. Stirring constantly, return to the boiling point. Lower the heat and simmer for five minutes. Cool the mixture and then refrigerate until ready to use.

2. When ready to serve, place mixed greens on each of six chilled plates. Alternate layers of avocado, grapefruit and red pepper in a fan shape atop the greens. Spoon approximately two tablespoons of the dressing over the salad and garnish with cilantro.

*TIPS
—Mixed greens are available at most groceries. They are conveniently washed and mixed so that you do not have to buy one head of each type of lettuce.

1 cup tequila
¼ cup chopped green chilies
1 tsp. cumin
salt
1 Tbl. honey
1 cup water
1 tsp. ground coriander
1 Tbl. orange juice
juice of 1 lime
1 Tbl. cornstarch mixed with
    2 Tbl. water
¾ lb. mixed greens (arugula,
    radicchio, etc.)*
3 avocados, peeled, seeded and
    sliced
2 pink grapefruits, sectioned
2 red bell peppers, roasted,
    peeled, seeded and cut into
    strips (see Before
    Beginning)
fresh cilantro to garnish

Chicken Breast Malanzani

Serves: Four to Six

Schmollinger suggests serving this healthy dish with rice or pasta and steamed cauliflower and broccoli seasoned with thyme and rosemary.

1 medium eggplant, peeled and cut into ¼" to ½" thick slices

flour

3 Tbl. olive oil plus additional as needed

6 chicken breast halves

1 tsp. fennel seeds

4 tomatoes, peeled, seeded and chopped (see Before Beginning)

4 oz. sun-dried tomatoes, chopped*

2 garlic cloves, minced

½ tsp. salt

1 cup dry Marsala wine

3 Tbl. minced fresh basil

1 Tbl. minced fresh oregano

8 oz. spinach

½ cup freshly grated Parmesan cheese

1. Dredge the eggplant in flour. In a large heavy skillet, heat two tablespoons of olive oil over medium-high heat and brown the eggplant on both sides. Remove the eggplant from the skillet and place on paper towels.

2. Dredge the chicken breasts in flour. Add one table-spoon of olive oil to the skillet used for the eggplant and brown the chicken on both sides over medium-high heat. Remove the chicken from the skillet and set aside.

3. Place a little more olive oil in the skillet and add the fennel seeds. Cook for a few seconds, stirring, then add the fresh and the sun-dried tomatoes, garlic, salt and wine. Cook, stirring, for five minutes, then return the chicken breasts to the skillet. Cover the skillet and cook the chicken, turning often, until done; five to 10 minutes.

4. Sprinkle the basil and oregano over the chicken and top with the spinach. Cover the skillet and remove from the heat. The spinach should be dark green, shiny and wilted after a few minutes. You may need to return the skillet to the heat if the spinach has not cooked enough. Serve on warm plates with the sauce spooned around the eggplant and chicken, and Parmesan sprinkled on top.

*TIPS
—If using dried sun-dried tomatoes, soak them in water for 30-60 minutes, until they are plumped and softened.

Chocolate-Raspberry Cake

Makes: One 2-layer 8" round cake (serves Eight)

A cup of freshly roasted coffee stirred with a cinnamon stick perfectly compliments the rich flavor of the dessert.

1. Preheat the oven to 350°. Spray two 8" round cake pans with cooking spray or coat with butter and then dust them with flour.*

2. Melt the chocolate, being careful not to scorch it. Set it aside to cool slightly.

3. In a mixing bowl, cream the butter and sugar until the mixture is light and smooth. One at a time, add the eggs, beating until well mixed. Add the chocolate and blend well.

4. Combine the milk and vanilla. Sift the flour, salt and baking powder. Alternately and in thirds, stir in the flour mixture and the milk mixture into the butter-egg mixture. Divide the batter between the two baking pans and bake for about 25 minutes. When done, the middle of the cake should spring back and not indent when gently pressed. Cool the cakes on a rack.

5. While the cake is cooling, prepare the icing. To assemble the cake, run a knife around the rim of each cake pan and turn the cakes out onto a tray or baking sheet. Place one cake on a plate. Spread a thick layer of raspberry jam on top of it. Place the second cake atop the first. Using a flat metal spatula, spread the icing

4 oz. semisweet chocolate
4 Tbl. unsalted butter
1⅔ cups sugar
3 large eggs, at room temperature
1 cup milk
1 tsp. vanilla
1½ cups flour
¼ tsp. salt
1 tsp. baking powder
1 small jar good-quality seedless raspberry jam
Chocolate Icing (recipe follows)
fresh raspberries to garnish
fresh mint to garnish

evenly over the top and sides of the cake. Garnish with fresh raspberries and mint leaves.

*TIPS
—Parchment paper is wonderful for lining baking pans. It's much better than a coating of butter and flour. If you use parchment, coat the pans with butter or oil first, then place the parchment (trace the pan to get the correct size and shape). If using parchment paper, you can omit the flour dusting. Parchment paper can be found in many groceries and most cookery shops.

Chocolate Icing

2 Tbl. butter
6 oz. semisweet chocolate
¾ cup sour cream
1 tsp. vanilla
⅓ cup heavy or whipping
        cream
2 Tbl. powdered
        (confectioners') sugar

In a heavy saucepan, melt the butter and chocolate, being careful not to scorch the chocolate. Remove the chocolate from the heat and pour it into a mixing bowl. Add the sour cream and blend well. In a separate bowl, mix the vanilla and cream. Alternately and in thirds, mix the cream mixture and the powdered sugar into the chocolate mixture. Beat until smooth.

Q's Restaurant

John Platt is one of a group of talented young chefs in Boulder. At Q's, his restaurant located on the mezzanine of the historic Boulderado Hotel, his touch can be seen everywhere, from the professional wait staff to the delicious American cuisine.

Platt, originally from New York, was trained at the Culinary Institute of America. After graduating, he moved to California where he met his wife. In 1988, they moved to Fort Collins. They loved the area, but Platt felt his options were limited there, so they moved to Connecticut where he worked on a degree in hotel and restaurant management. However, the Platts dreamed of returning to the West. "We really wanted to come back to Colorado," says Platt. "We love the mountains and we had friends in Boulder, so we decided to come here."

Platt's story reads like a Boulder culinary family tree with the former Marbles restaurant at its root. Marbles was owned by Mark Shockley (now of The Harvest) and Dave Berenson (now of Daily Bread). David Query, the founder of Q's, was filling in for vacationing Berenson when Platt met him. That meeting led to the fulfillment of Platt's dream to run his own restaurant. "I've been lucky to hook up with good people," says Platt. When Marbles closed, Query was in the process of opening Q's and he hired Platt as his sous chef. In 1993, Platt bought him out and Query went on to open Zolo Grill and later Jax Fishhouse.

Platt admits, "This place has been good to me." Still, he has worked hard for his success. "I think personal attention is a big part of it," he explains. "I don't write a menu and say to my staff, 'This is how you make it, now go make it.' I'm in the kitchen five nights a week."

The menu at Q's changes monthly to take advantage of the freshest seasonal ingredients. Platt has a talent for creating interesting combinations with textures and tastes that complement each other. An example is an appetizer of juniper-grilled Georgia quail on a bed

John Platt, Chef/Owner

2115 13th Street
Boulderado Hotel
Boulder
444-5232

of cumin slaw with blueberry vinaigrette topped with fried carrot strings. Entrées include fish and seafood items, such as grilled sea scallops with red curry, papaya and coconut, and poultry and meat, such as grilled veal chops with sweet potato spaetzle and nutmeg jus. The menu always contains a vegetarian offering as well.

Buttermilk Fried Chicken with Romaine and BBQ Dressing

2 cups flour

1 tsp. cayenne

1 tsp. white pepper

1 tsp. ground cumin

12 oz. of chicken breasts cut into 12 equal strips, or 12 tenderloin portions from chicken breasts with tendon removed

1½ cups buttermilk

3 cups fresh white breadcrumbs

3 cups canola oil (or other vegetable oil)

1 large head romaine lettuce, washed, dried and torn into large pieces

1 Granny Smith apple, peeled (optional), cored and thinly sliced

2 cups seedless red grape halves

3 stalks celery, sliced thinly on the slant or bias

1 cup barbecue sauce (a spicy one is best)

¾ cup buttermilk

¼ cup half-and-half

Serves: Six

This is a great light supper or luncheon dish. The greens are tossed with apples, grapes and celery and topped with chicken fillets.

1. Mix the flour and seasonings. Dredge the breasts in the seasoned flour, then dip them in the buttermilk. Coat the chicken with the breadcrumbs. Heat at least 1" of oil in a wide, deep pan until it reaches 350°; do not over-heat. Cook the chicken in the oil in batches until golden brown and cooked through. Drain the chicken on paper towels.

2. Toss the romaine and half of the apples, grapes and celery with the dressing. Divide among six plates. Place two pieces of chicken per plate on top of the romaine and sprinkle with the remaining apples, grapes and celery. Serve immediately.

3. For the Creamy BBQ Dressing, whisk barbecue sauce, buttermilk, and half-and-half together. Drizzle over chicken and romaine.

Spinach and Oyster Mushroom Cakes

Serves: Six

This dish is great as an appetizer, vegetarian entrée or as a side dish with grilled fish, poultry or game. You can substitute other wild mushrooms and/or greens. The roasted peppers need to marinate for at least four hours.

1. In a large skillet over high heat, heat one tablespoon of the olive oil and then cook the oyster mushrooms over high heat until soft. Add the garlic and shallots and cook for two minutes more. Season to taste with salt and pepper. Remove from the pan and cool.

2. To the same pan, add one tablespoon of the olive oil. When the oil is hot, sear the spinach until just wilted. Season to taste with salt and pepper and set aside.

3. In a large bowl, mix the mushrooms and spinach with the bread crumbs, sage and egg. Use some of the mixture to make a ¾"-thick round cake about 2½" to 3" in diameter. Heat one tablespoon of olive oil in the skillet over high heat. Dredge the cake in flour and cook for four minutes on each side. If the cake doesn't hold together well, add an additional egg to the mixture before forming, dredging and cooking the remaining cakes.

4. Divide the garlic purée between six warm plates. Place the cakes in the center of the purée. Top with the roasted peppers and feta.

3 Tbl. olive oil
1 lb. oyster mushrooms, stems
     removed, cut in half
1 garlic clove, minced
1 shallot, minced
salt and pepper
1 lb. spinach, rinsed well, tough
     stems removed
1 cup fresh white breadcrumbs
2 leaves fresh sage, cut into thin
     strips
1 large egg, lightly beaten
flour for dredging
Roasted Garlic Purée (recipe
     on page 140)
Roasted Peppers in Balsamic
     Vinegar (recipe on page
     140)
6 oz. feta cheese, crumbled

Roasted Garlic Purée

12 large garlic cloves, peeled
¼ cup chopped onion
olive oil
pinch of saffron
1 Tbl. flour
1½ cups chicken broth
salt and white pepper

In a saucepan over medium heat, sauté the garlic and onion in olive oil until golden brown and soft. Add the saffron and flour. Stir for five minutes to cook the flour. Whisk in the chicken broth. Bring to a simmer and cook for 15 minutes. Purée in the blender until very smooth. Add salt and white pepper to taste.

Roasted Peppers in Balsamic Vinegar

2 red bell peppers
1 yellow bell pepper
salt and pepper
2 Tbl. balsamic vinegar
1 Tbl. olive oil

Place the peppers on a foil-lined baking sheet. Broil, turning, until they are evenly charred and blistered. Seal the peppers in a brown paper bag and let let steam for 10 minutes. Peel and seed the peppers and cut them into ¼" strips. Season the peppers with a little salt and pepper. Place the peppers in a bowl and toss with the vinegar and olive oil. Refrigerate for at least four hours before using.

Grilled Asparagus Salad with Oven-Dried Tomatoes

Serves: Six

9 Roma tomatoes, halved
    lengthwise
olive oil
balsamic vinegar
¼ cup minced fresh herbs
    (thyme, basil, oregano, etc.)
salt and pepper
ice water
2 bundles asparagus, cut to an
    equal length.
½ lb. arugula, stems removed,
    rinsed well
Balsamic Vinaigrette (recipe
    follows)
6 large slices rustic-style bread
6 oz. blue cheese, crumbled

1. Preheat the oven to 275°. Place the tomato halves on a cookie sheet cut-sides up and sprinkle them with olive oil, balsamic vinegar, fresh herbs, and salt and pepper to taste. Bake the tomatoes for two hours. Remove the tomatoes from the oven and cool.

2. Fill a medium bowl with ice water and set aside. Fill a medium saucepan with water and add ½ tsp. of salt. Bring to a boil. Place the asparagus in the boiling water and cook for two minutes. Drain the asparagus and immediately plunge into ice water to stop the cooking and keep their bright color. Drain and set aside.

3. Prepare the grill. Toss the arugula with just enough vinaigrette to coat the leaves. Divide it among six plates. Brush the asparagus and bread with a little olive oil. Season the asparagus with a little salt and pepper and grill it lightly (until al dente), along with the bread slices.

4. Arrange the roasted tomatoes and asparagus spears atop the greens on each plate. Top with cheese and drizzle a little vinaigrette around the plate. Set the grilled bread on the side of the plate and serve.

Balsamic Vinaigrette

½ cup balsamic vinegar
1 cup olive oil
1 tsp. minced shallot
½ tsp. minced garlic
salt and pepper

Whisk all of the ingredients together.

Chile Crusted Red Trout on Cornbread and Chard

6 (6 oz.) fillets red trout or
    coho salmon, skin on
olive oil
salt and pepper
ground cumin
New Mexico chile powder*
4 oz. applewood-smoked bacon
    or other good bacon,
    chopped into ½" pieces
2 Tbl. minced shallots
½ cup + 2 Tbl. sherry vinegar
1¼ cups chicken broth
2 cups cubed stale corn bread,
    cut into ¾" cubes
2 cups roughly chopped chard
3 Tbl. salted butter
2 cups succotash (any
    combination of corn, peas,
    sugar snap peas, fava
    beans and/or diced green
    and green wax beans)
4 Tbl. unsalted butter
1-2 Tbl. chopped chives

Serves: Six

1. Brush the trout with a little olive oil, sprinkle with salt and pepper, and season generously with cumin and chile powder.

2. In a large skillet, cook the bacon until crisp. Drain most of the grease, add the shallots and cook until golden brown. Add the vinegar and broth, stirring constantly. Boil until reduced by half. Add salt and pepper to taste.

3. In another large skillet, cook the cornbread and chard in the salted butter until the chard is softened. You can add a little broth to the cornbread mixture to soften it a little. Add salt, pepper, cumin and chile powder to taste.

4. Cook the succotash in a saucepan with a little water and butter until al dente Season with salt and pepper.

5. Whisk the four tablespoons of unsalted butter and the chives into the simmering bacon vinaigrette.

6. To serve, place piles of the cornbread mixture in the center of warm plates. Quickly grill or pan-fry the trout until done to your taste. Halve the trout on the diagonal and rest it against the cornbread mixture. Spoon bacon vinaigrette over and around the trout. Spoon the succotash onto the plate next to the trout. Serve immediately.

*TIPS
—New Mexico chile powder is not the same as the chili powder found in the spice aisle. Chile powder is made from dried, ground, red New Mexico chiles. It is available in the Mexican food aisle of most groceries.

142

Ahi Tuna with Wild Rice Cakes and Curried Pumpkin Butter

Serves: Six

This unusual combination of flavors is delicious. Prepare the pumpkin butter while the wild rice is cooking. When the rice cakes are done, have someone grill the tuna while you sear the vegetables. This way everything will be ready to assemble as soon as the tuna is done.

1. For the rice cakes, combine the rice, water, bay leaves, ginger, garlic, onion, cumin and coriander in a medium saucepan. Bring to a boil, then lower the heat to a simmer and cook the rice until the grains burst; about 40 minutes. Drain the rice and remove the bay leaves, ginger, garlic and onion. Cool.

1 cup wild rice*
2 quarts water
3 bay leaves
3 slices peeled gingerroot
4 garlic cloves, peeled and
     slightly crushed
½ medium onion
1 tsp. cumin seeds
1 tsp. coriander seeds
1 egg
½ cup flour
salt and pepper
canola oil

2. Place the cooled rice in a mixing bowl. Beat with a mixer on high speed for five minutes. Add the egg and flour and blend well. Add salt and pepper to taste. Shape into ¾"-thick, 3"cakes. Coat the bottom of a skillet with canola oil. Heat the oil and then add the rice cakes. Cook until crisp and brown on both sides. Cover loosely with foil to keep warm.

3. To make curried pumpkin butter, boil the chicken stock in a small saucepan until it has been reduced to one cup. Add the pumpkin purée and curry paste. Bring to a simmer and gradually whisk in the butter, one piece at a time.

2 cups chicken stock
½ cup pumpkin purée*
1 tsp. red curry paste*
6 Tbl. butter, cut into 6 pieces

6 (5oz.) Ahi tuna steaks
olive oil
salt and pepper
1 cup shitake mushrooms,
     stems removed, sliced
1 cup bok choy, sliced,* use
     white part only
¼ cup sliced red bell peppers
¼ cup sliced yellow bell
     peppers
2 Tbl. canola oil
2 Tbl. soy sauce mixed with 3
     drops sesame oil
sweet soy sauce*
½ cup toasted pumpkin seeds

For the tuna:

4. Prepare the grill. Brush each tuna steak with olive oil and season it with salt and pepper. Grill to your liking (medium-rare to medium is recommended).

5. In a hot skillet or wok, quickly sear the mushrooms, bok choy and peppers in the canola oil. Add the soy sauce mixture and red pepper flakes. Season with salt and pepper.

6. On warm plates, arrange the tuna with a few rice cakes and the stir-fried vegetables. Drizzle pumpkin butter around each plate and squirt a few curly lines of sweet soy sauce in a decorative pattern around each plate. Sprinkle with toasted pumpkin seeds and serve.

*TIPS
—Wild rice is found in the rice or gourmet section of the grocery. If buying it in bulk, be sure to clean it well first by soaking it in several inches of water. Stir the water and rice a little and then let it sit for a few minutes. Any debris will come to the surface, the rice will sink to the bottom. Skim any debris, drain and it's ready to cook.
—Be sure to buy plain pumpkin purée, not pumpkin that is seasoned for pie.
—Red curry paste is found in most Asian markets and the Asian section of many groceries.
—Bok choy is also known as Chinese white cabbage or white mustard cabbage. It looks like celery with dark green leaves. It is available at most groceries.
—Sweet soy sauce can be found in Asian markets and some groceries. An easy way to squirt it is to place it in an empty yellow mustard bottle with a squirt top.

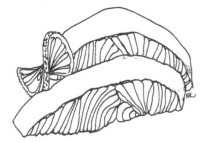

In 1983 Shanti Awatramani moved to Boulder from New York City and opened the Royal Peacock. Awatramani's family was in the restaurant business in India, so he had gained extensive instruction in the kitchen while growing up. Awatramani moved to New York from India when he was 18. Explaining his move he says, "My father had a guru. When my father died, the guru sent me here to make money. I did not want to make money, I just wanted to have a good time." What brought him to Colorado? "Destiny," he states. "Everything is planned according to your karma."

A visit to the Royal Peacock's kitchen reveals an entirely different kind of space than you will find in most restaurants. One wall is taken up by a tandoori, the traditional Indian clay oven fired with hot coals. The line cook flattens the dough for naan (an East Indian, white flour flat bread) and slaps it onto the inside wall of the oven about a foot from the intensely hot embers, leaving you to wonder how he escapes burning his hands. Then he moistens the edges of poppadums (a wafer-thin, disk-shaped, cracker-like bread made with lentil flour) and pushes the moistened end against the inside edge of the clay oven. Soon, the poppadums begin to puff up and crisp.

In another part of the kitchen, chef-owner Awatramani is stirring onions, garlic and jalapeños in a huge wok that is only four feet off of the floor. He stirs the mixture with what looks like a small snow shovel. Soon, the aroma from the wok makes your mouth water and you rush out of the kitchen to find a table and order.

It's best to bring friends to the Royal Peacock so you can sample several items. Crisp poppadums accompanied by a fresh mint and a pomegranate sauce

Royal Peacock

Shanti K. Awatramani, Chef/Owner

5290 Arapahoe Road, Greenwood Plaza, Boulder
447-1409

made in-house, are brought to the table as soon as you are seated (jars of the sauce are sometimes available for sale).

Opening the menu, one discovers delicious appetizers such as samosas (delicate, deep-fried pastries filled with potatoes and peas or a spicy mutton mixture). Numerous vegetarian dishes are offered in addition to curries, tandoori chicken and meats served sizzling on a bed of onions, yogurt and chutneys. Breads such as naan and paratha (a flaky, fried east Indian bread made with whole-wheat flour) complement the savory offerings.

Awatramani lives in Louisville with his wife, son and daughter, but he spends most of his time at the restaurant. You can usually find him, a scarf tied around his head, in the kitchen or at the door greeting customers. When greeting diners, Awatramani gestures toward the dining room with his hand and says, "When you are at the Peacock, you are in India."

Raita

1 cucumber, peeled and sliced in half lengthwise
1 tsp. salt, plus more as needed
1 Tbl. minced onion
1 tomato, peeled and chopped (see Before Beginning)
1 Tbl. chopped cilantro
1 cup plain yogurt
1½ tsp. cumin
salt and pepper
sprigs of cilantro to garnish

1. Seed the cucumber with a spoon, then cut it into ½" pieces. Mix the cucumbers with the salt and let sit for 10 minutes. Drain the liquid that has accumulated from the cucumbers. Add the onion, tomato and cilantro to the cucumbers. Combine the yogurt and cumin and add to the cucumbers. Mix well.

2. Chill the raita, covered, in the refrigerator until ready to serve. Before serving, add salt and pepper to taste. Serve the raita in individual bowls or pass in a large bowl. Garnish with sprigs of cilantro and a slice of cucumber.

Madras Fish and Egg Curry

Serves: Four as an entree or Six as part of a
               multi-course meal

In India, this dish is often made as an egg curry by
omitting the fish. Egg curry can be served as part of a
brunch buffet. If you have never prepared Indian dishes,
this is a good one to try because it is so simple.

1. Preheat the oven to 350°. Heat the ghee or oil in a
large saucepan over medium heat. Add the onion and
garlic, and cook until soft. Add the coriander, cumin,
turmeric, ginger, chili powder and pepper. Stirring
constantly, cook the mixture for two minutes. If you are
using fish, add it now. Stir the fish around so that it
flakes into pieces as it cooks. Cook until the fish is no
longer translucent.

2. Place the coconut and water in a blender and blend
for two minutes, or until the mixture is liquefied, using
the blender's highest speed. Stir the tomato paste into the
onion mixture over medium heat. Add the coconut
mixture to the onion mixture, and bring it to a boil. Add
the lemon juice and salt. Lower the heat to simmer.

3. Halve the hard-boiled eggs lengthwise and arrange
them in a shallow baking dish, cut side down. Pour the
onion mixture over the eggs and cover with aluminum
foil. Bake for 10 minutes. Serve immediately.

*TIPS
—Ghee is very similar to clarified butter (see Before
Beginning).

¼ cup ghee or vegetable oil*
1 large onion, sliced
1 garlic clove, sliced
1 tsp. ground coriander
2 tsp. ground cumin
1 tsp. powdered turmeric
½ tsp. ground ginger
1 tsp. chili powder
1 tsp. black pepper
4 oz. whitefish (optional)
4 oz. dried, unsweetened,
    shredded or flaked
    coconut
1 cup warm water
2 Tbl. tomato paste
juice of 1 lemon
1 tsp. salt
6 eggs, hard-boiled and peeled

Duck Vindaloo

Serves   Four

This is a classic southern Indian dish. Awatramani suggests using wild duck if available. Serve the duck with any kind of rice. Curries improve with age, so you can make this dish in the morning and reheat it for dinner.

½ cup ghee (see "clarifying butter" in Before Beginning) or vegetable oil

2½-3 lbs. duck, washed well and cut into 8 pieces

2 large onions, thinly sliced

4 garlic cloves, thinly sliced

1 tsp. red pepper flakes

4 whole cloves

4 whole cardamom seeds

2 tsp. powdered turmeric

2 tsp. whole coriander seeds

1 tsp. whole cumin seeds

2 tsp. poppy seeds

2 tsp. ground black pepper

4 Tbl. white vinegar

1 tsp. salt

2 cups chicken broth

4 green chiles, seeded, ribs removed and minced*

2 oz. dried, unsweetened, shredded or flaked coconut

1. Heat the ghee or oil over high heat in a large heavy saucepan. Quickly brown the duck on all sides. Remove the duck from the pan and set aside. Lower the heat to medium. Add the onions and garlic, and cook until they begin to soften.

2. Add the red pepper flakes, cloves and cardamom, and cook, stirring, for one minute. Add the turmeric, coriander, cumin, poppy seeds and pepper. Cook, continuously stirring for two minutes. Add the vinegar, salt and broth. Bring the mixture to a boil. Return the duck pieces to the pan, lower the heat to a simmer and cook for one hour.

3. Add the chiles and coconut. Cook for another 10 to 15 minutes, until the duck is tender. Remove the duck, reserving the liquid in the pan. Place the duck on a heated, deep platter or serving dish. Strain the liquid from the saucepan and then pour it over the duck. Serve immediately.

*TIPS
—If you like spicy food, use jalapeños. If not, use a milder green chili, such as an Anaheim or poblano.
—Raita, a combination of yogurt and cucumber, is a nice side dish to serve with Indian food (recipe on p. 146).

Coconut Lamb

Serves: Four to Six

Awatramani says, "The combination of spicy lamb curry with coconut results in a dish so wonderful you have to taste it to believe it."

1. Preheat the oven to 400°. Cut about one-third of the coconut pulp into slivers and arrange them on a baking sheet. Place the cardamom, cloves, coriander, cumin and cinnamon stick on a second baking sheet. Place both baking sheets in the oven and roast for 20 minutes, turning the coconut until it is evenly browned on all sides. Remove the baking sheets from the oven and set them aside.

2. Cut the remaining coconut into small pieces. Place the reserved coconut milk in a blender. With the blender on high speed, slow add the pieces of coconut. When all of the coconut has been blended, add the hot water and blend for one minute. Set aside.

3. In a large bowl, toss the lamb with the lemon juice, salt and pepper. Set aside.

4. In a large saucepan, heat the ghee, clarified butter, or oil over medium heat. Add the onions and garlic, and cook until soft, stirring occasionally. Add the turmeric and ginger, and stir. Remove the pan from the heat.

5. Divide the roasted spices from step one between two brown paper bags. Using a rolling pin, crush the spices by pushing the rolling pin over the top of the paper sack. Transfer the crushed spices to a blender or grinder and

1 large coconut, broken in two, milk reserved*
4 whole cardamom seeds
4 whole cloves
1 Tbl. whole coriander seeds
1 tsp. whole cumin seeds
1 2" cinnamon stick
1 cup hot water
2 lbs. lamb, cut into 1" cubes
juice of 2 lemons
2 tsp. salt
2 tsp. pepper
½ cup ghee, vegetable oil, or clarified butter (see page xvi)
2 large onions, minced
3 garlic cloves, peeled and sliced
1 tsp. ground turmeric
1 tsp. ground ginger
½ tsp. red pepper flakes

process them until pulverized. Add the spice mixture from the blender and the red pepper flakes to the onion mixture in the saucepan. Over low heat, stir to blend well.

6. Add the lamb to the onion mixture and stir until the lamb cubes are well coated with the onion mixture. Raise the heat to high, add the coconut milk mixture to the onion and lamb mixture and bring it to a boil. Lower the heat and simmer until the lamb is tender and done. To serve, pile lamb onto a heated deep platter and top with the sauce. Sprinkle with the toasted coconut slivers from step one and serve.

*TIPS

—Coconuts can be found year-round in supermarkets, but are most commonly available from October to December. Avoid coconuts with moldy or wet "eyes." To extract the milk, pound a nail or skewer into the eyes of the coconut. Drain the milk into a bowl. It takes a while for all of the milk to drain. Place the coconut in a 350° oven and bake for about 10 minutes, or until it is very hot. While it is still hot, open the shell by pounding the coconut with a hammer or mallet around its middle. Pry out the coconut meat with a small paring knife. Peel off any skin remaining on the pieces.

The Silver Palace is not the stereotypical Chinese restaurant. The menu does not have a multitude of pages, the decor is fine dining with white tablecloths and fine china, the food is slightly different and more elegant than the usual Szechwan/Hunan cuisine. It is difficult to put into words, but one visit to the Silver Palace and you will understand why it is so special.

Inspired by the New York City restaurant Shun Lee Palace, Nang Ng, his brother, Ting, and four friends, who had grown up in the same Bronx apartment building, hatched the idea for the Silver Palace. Shun Lee Palace was a pioneer of Szechwan/Hunan cuisine. It was the first Chinese restaurant to receive four stars from the restaurant critic at *The New York Times*. Ting Ng was a waiter at the Shun Lee Palace.

They opened their first restaurant in New Jersey, but soon realized that their concept would not work in that area. They looked for a location with fewer Chinese restaurants. "We chose Burlington, Vermont, because there were no Chinese restaurants there and the economy was good," says Ting. The decision proved to be a good one. The restaurant did well, and soon the partners were thinking about opening another one.

"We liked the weather in Florida and Fort Lauderdale seemed to be a great location," says Nang. Nang stayed in Vermont to oversee the first restaurant while some of his partners moved to Florida to open the second.

They selected Boulder for their third endeavor. Nang says, "Boulder reminded us of Burlington. It's smaller and a university town. Also the growth and economy are really good here." The partners also liked the idea of a big city being within a half hour's drive. The partners picked a space that had formerly housed several Italian restaurants. "It's not the greatest location," admits Nang, "but the space was right and the parking is good."

Silver Palace Restaurant

*Nang Ng,
Co-owner*

3100 Arapahoe Avenue,
Boulder
447-3828

The menu has evolved from popular specials at the other two restaurants. A favorite appetizer, Hunan Popcorn (spicy, deep-fried calamari) was inspired by Paul Prudhomme's Cajun Popcorn. The menu also offers items such as Crispy Pork Grand Marnier (pork tenderloin dusted with Lotus flour, in a garlic-Grand Marnier sauce) or Chicken Gwin Jin, sliced breast of chicken grilled in a wok and sautéed in rice wine, garlic and aged mushroom soy sauce.

Hot and Sour Soup

Serves: Four to Six

This soup may be served as part of a Chinese meal, but is also great for a simple supper with some bread and an Asian Green Salad (see recipe on page 154).

6 dried mushrooms, stems removed (the Chinese variety is best)
warm water
6 cups chicken broth
1 Tbl. soy sauce
½ cup thinly sliced, canned bamboo shoots
¼ lb. pork, cut into thin slivers
¼ tsp. white pepper, or more to taste
3 Tbl. white vinegar
1 cup ½" cubes firm tofu
2 Tbl. cornstarch mixed with 3 Tbl. water
1 egg beaten with 2½ tsp. Oriental sesame oil
salt, pepper, soy sauce and/or vinegar to taste
chopped green onion to garnish

1. Soak the dried mushrooms in warm water for 30 minutes. Drain the mushrooms and thinly slice them.

2. In a large saucepan, combine the mushrooms, broth, soy sauce, bamboo shoots, pork, pepper and vinegar. Bring to a boil. Skim any residue from the surface of the soup. Lower the heat to a simmer and add the tofu. Simmer the soup, uncovered, for 20 minutes. You can make the soup ahead of time to this point.

3. Just before serving the soup, add the cornstarch mixture and turn up the heat. Stir constantly until the soup thickens slightly. When the soup is boiling, gradually add the egg mixture. Add salt, pepper, soy sauce and/or vinegar to taste. Ladle the soup into warm bowls and sprinkle green onion on top. Serve immediately.

Grilled Chicken Breasts Glazed with Honey-Mustard

Serves: Four

This is a very simple dish; it's great for a day when there's little time to cook. Serve it with rice and a salad or vegetable, such as Stir-Fried Asparagus (recipe follows). The glaze can be made a day in advance.

1. Place the chicken in a bowl and cover it with the rice wine. Marinate the chicken for at least one hour, and as long as two hours.

2. In a small bowl, combine the soy sauce, honey and mustard, and whisk until blended well.

3. Drain the chicken and pat it dry with paper towels. Brush the chicken with a little olive oil. Grill over high heat for one minute and then turn it. Baste liberally with the soy sauce mixture. Cook for one minute, then turn and baste again. Repeat the turning, basting and cooking until you have reached a total cooking time of five minutes. Test for doneness and cook longer if necessary, using the same turning and basting method, being careful not to overcook the chicken (or it will dry out).

4. Remove the chicken from the grill and allow it to sit for a few minutes. Then slice and divide it among warm plates.

4 chicken breast halves
1 cup rice wine (sake), or ½
    cup sherry combined with
    ½ cup dry white wine
¼ cup soy sauce
2 Tbl. + 2 tsp. honey
4 tsp. dry mustard
olive oil

Stir-Fried Asparagus with Almonds

Serves: Four

1 bundle of asparagus
2 Tbl. canola oil
½ cup slivered almonds
large pinch of sugar
large pinch of salt
4 green onions, coarsely
chopped

1. Cut each asparagus spear on the diagonal into three or four pieces. If the stems are thick, trim 1" from the bottoms, or peel the stems.

2. In a heavy skillet or wok, heat one tablespoon of the oil. When the oil is very hot, stir-fry the almonds for about one minute, until lightly browned. Remove the almonds with a slotted spoon and drain on paper towels.

3. Heat the other one tablespoon of oil in the wok. Add the asparagus and stir-fry for one minute. Add the sugar and salt. Continue stirring for another few minutes, or until the asparagus is almost done to your liking. Add the green onions and stir-fry until the asparagus is done. Serve immediately.

Asian Green Salad

Serves: Four to Six

1 lb. mixed greens, including
    iceberg lettuce (for its
    crispness)
1 carrot, peeled and sliced
⅔ cup blanched pea pods
3 green onions, sliced
¼ cup soy sauce
¼ cup sugar
1 Tbl. Dijon mustard
¾ cup white vinegar
1 cup canola oil

1. Toss the mixed greens, carrots, pea pods and onions together in a large salad bowl.

2. Combine the soy sauce, sugar, mustard, vinegar and oil in a jar, close the lid tightly and shake. (This recipe makes about two cups of dressing. The dressing will keep in the refrigerator for several weeks.) Add just enough dressing to the salad bowl to coat the greens and vegetables, and toss.

Gwin Jin Shrimp

Serves: Two

Ng recommends serving the shrimp on a bed of steamed or sauteed vegetables. You can substitute bite-size pieces of salmon or chicken for the shrimp.

1. Combine the soy sauce, oyster sauce, sherry, brown sugar and honey, and blend well. Set aside.

2. Heat the oil in a large skillet or wok and then add the shrimp. Cook, stirring constantly, for 90 seconds. Add the garlic and continue to cook, stirring, for 1½ more minutes. Add the soy sauce mixture and cook for a few more minutes, until the shrimp are cooked through and pink. Serve immediately.

*TIPS
—Aged mushroom soy sauce and oyster sauce can be found in Asian markets.

2 Tbl. aged mushroom soy
   sauce*
1 Tbl. oyster sauce*
¼ cup + 2 Tbl. sherry
1 Tbl. brown sugar
1 Tbl. honey
1 Tbl. vegetable oil
12 oz. large shrimp or prawns,
   peeled and deveined
3 garlic cloves, minced

Pete Steinhauer

University of Colorado Regent

Vietnam has become a family affair for the Steinhauers. The Army sent Pete Steinhauer to Vietnam in 1966. While there, he became fascinated with the country, its people and its food. He was determined to return to Vietnam after the war. When Vietnam opened its doors to tourists in 1989, Steinhauer was one of the first visitors. He has since returned five times, often taking his family with him.

The Steinhauers do not just tour the country, they participate. Steinhauer founded an organization called the "Friendship Bridge," which sends doctors, nurses and medical supplies to Vietnamese clinics. It also brings Vietnamese medical personnel to the United States for supplemental training. Steinhauer's wife Julianne has spent many hours working in the clinics. One of his daughters produced a rock concert in Da Nang. His son has taken hauntingly beautiful photographs of the Vietnamese people, which were exhibited in Denver throughout the summer of 1996.

The Steinhauers' efforts in Vietnam have led to many friendships—one resulted in their sponsorship of a young Vietnamese exchange student, Nhu Nhu. Nhu Nhu could barely speak a word of English when she arrived. Now she is a student in international relations at the University of Colorado and a sorority member. She is the first exchange student from Vietnam to be educated in the United States since 1954.

Steinhauer collected many Vietnamese recipes while traveling around the country and has become an expert at cooking these dishes. He has prepared a number of special Vietnamese dinners for the "Festival of Dinners," series—events benefiting the Colorado Music Festival. He makes spring rolls with nuoc cham sauce, served with bean sprouts, cilantro, rice noodles and mint; Hanoi beef and noodle soup; pork in coconut milk; and steamed chicken with ginger and rice. He follows the dinners with an amusing and educational slide show entitled "Vietnam: Then and Now." He claims he is not in the kitchen very much these days because he has been "out-classed." "Nhu Nhu has taken over as far as Vietnamese cooking is concerned," says Steinhauer. "She is a fabulous cook."

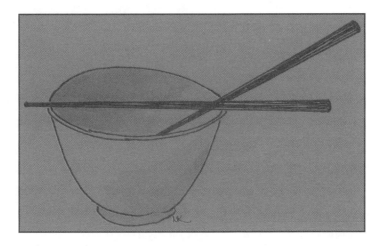

Vietnamese Egg Rolls

Serves: Twelve as an appetizer or
Six as part of a Vietnamese dinner

2 Tbl. canola oil
½ lb. boneless pork, minced
¼ lb. shrimp, shelled and
    minced
1 tsp. minced garlic
1 cup chopped green onion
1 cup shredded carrot*
4-5 oz. rice sticks,* soaked in
    warm water for 30 minutes
    and drained
6 cloud ears,* soaked in warm
    water for 30 minutes,
    drained and minced
1 tsp. pepper
1 egg
1 tsp. water
1 package rice paper egg roll
    skins
canola oil for deep frying
Bibb or leaf lettuce
fresh mint and cilantro leaves
fresh bean sprouts, blanched
    for 10 seconds and
    refreshed in cold water
extra rice sticks, soaked in
    warm water for 30 minutes
    and drained
Nuoc Cham Sauce (recipe
    follows)

1. In a wok or skillet, heat the canola oil until it is very hot. Add the pork, shrimp, garlic, onion and carrot. Over high heat, cook, stirring constantly, until the pork and shrimp are just done. Remove the mixture to a bowl and cool slightly. Add the rice sticks, cloud ears and pepper, and mix thoroughly.

2. Beat one egg with one teaspoon of water and set aside. Place one rice paper skin at a time in water until it softens. Pat dry and then place one heaping teaspoon of the pork-shrimp mixture near one of the curved ends. Roll once so that the mixture is covered with the rice paper skin. Spread a small amount of the egg mixture on the remaining edges of the rice skin. Fold over the sides then roll forward the rest of the way. You should have a long thin tube. Repeat with each rice paper skin until all the filling has been used. The egg rolls can be covered and refrigerated for up to one day in advance at this point.

3. Preheat the oven to 275°. Heat about 6" of oil in a wok or skillet; the temperature should reach 275° to 285° before beginning frying. Carefully slide some of the egg rolls down the side of the wok (or gently place them in the skillet), one at a time, being careful not to crowd them or they will stick together. Cook the rolls for about five minutes, turning once, until they are golden brown on all sides. Fry the rolls in batches. When done, remove the rolls from the oil and drain on paper towels. Keep the cooked rolls warm in the oven until ready to serve.

4. To serve, arrange lettuce, mint, cilantro, bean sprouts and rice sticks on a large serving platter. Place the egg rolls

in the center. To eat, wrap an egg roll in a lettuce leaf and top with mint, cilantro, sprouts and rice sticks, as desired. Roll up, dip in nuoc cham sauce and eat soft taco-style.

Nuoc Cham Sauce

Combine the sugar, water, vinegar, garlic and salt in a saucepan and bring to a boil. Lower the heat and simmer for 20 minutes. Add the chile paste, carrot and red pepper flakes. Cook one minute and cool.

*TIPS
—To shred carrots, use a cheese grater or food processor.
—Rice sticks (also called rice vermicelli), cloud ears, rice paper egg roll skins and chile paste with garlic may be found in Asian markets or the Asian section of the grocery.
—To blanch bean sprouts, plunge them in boiling water for 10 seconds, drain and then place in ice water to stop the cooking.
—The nuoc cham sauce calls for one tablespoon of red pepper flakes, which sounds like a lot. You will be disappointed, however, if you do not follow the recipe.

1 cup sugar
½ cup water
½ cup white vinegar
1 tsp. minced garlic
1 tsp. salt
2 tsp. chile paste with garlic*
a couple of Tbl. shredded carrot*
1 Tbl. red pepper flakes*

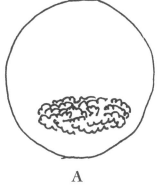

A

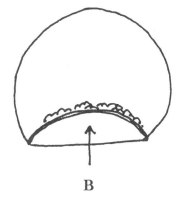

B

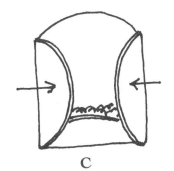

C

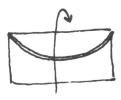

D

159

Vietnamese Pork with Coconut

Serves: Six

Can be made up to one day in advance and reheated.

2 lbs. boneless pork roast
salt and pepper
2 Tbl. canola oil
½ cup minced onion
2 Tbl. minced garlic
2 Tbl. minced gingerroot
2 Tbl. sambal oelek*
¾ cup soy sauce
1 Tbl. sugar
1 (14 oz.) can coconut milk*

steamed rice for six

1. Lightly season the pork with salt and pepper. Heat the oil in a heavy casserole dish or pot, such as a Dutch oven, and brown the pork on all sides in the oil. Remove the pork and set it aside.

2. Pour off most of the fat that accumulated in the casserole. Add the onion, garlic, ginger and sambal oelek to the casserole. Cook, stirring constantly, over medium heat for one minute. Add the soy sauce, sugar and coconut milk and stir until the sugar dissolves. Bring to a boil.

3. Return the pork to the pan and simmer slowly in the coconut milk mixture until tender; approximately one hour. Add salt and pepper to taste. Remove the pork from the pan and slice. Place slices of pork on steamed rice and spoon the sauce over it. Pass the remaining sauce.

*TIPS
—Sambal oelek is an Asian condiment of chile paste, often mixed with brown sugar and salt. It is available in Asian markets and the Asian section of some groceries.
—Coconut milk can be found in the Asian section of most groceries.

Pete's Old Fashioned Peach Pie

Serves: Six to Eight

1. Preheat the oven to 350°. Prepare a crust for a deep-dish pie pan. Combine the brown sugar, granulated sugar and flour. Rub or cut the butter into the sugar to make a crumbly mixture. Place half of the mixture in the bottom of the pie crust.

2. Arrange the peaches on top of the sugar mixture. Top the peaches with the remaining sugar mixture and evenly pour the cream over the top. The filling should be at least 1" from the top of the pie pan.

3. Bake for one hour or more, until the crust is brown. The pie may seem runny. Allow it to sit for at least one hour before serving. It is best served warm with vanilla ice cream.

1 deep-dish pie crust, unbaked (Food Processor Pastry recipe follows)
½ cup packed brown sugar
½ cup granulated sugar
2 Tbl. flour
2 Tbl. butter, cut into small pieces
4-5 fresh peaches, peeled, pitted and sliced
½ cup old-fashioned heavy cream

Food Processor Pastry

Makes: One 8" to 10" deep-dish pie crust

Place the flour, sugar and salt in a food processor. Cut the butter into eight or more pieces and add it to the flour mixture. Turn the processor on and off several times (pulse) until the butter is pea-sized. Sprinkle the ice-cold water over the mixture and process for 10 seconds. If the mixture is beginning to stick together when you pinch it between your fingers, stop processing. If the mixture is too dry and crumbly, add more ice water in very small amounts. Process for five seconds after each addition and test by pinching the dough between your fingers each time. Remove the dough from the processor and knead it a few times. If the dough is not being used immediately, wrap it tightly in plastic wrap and refrigerate. Bring the dough back to room temperature before rolling it out.

2 cups all-purpose flour
2 Tbl. sugar
½ tsp. salt
1 stick cold butter
3 Tbl. ice-cold water

Treppeda's Gourmet Market

Howard Treppeda and Carl Smith, Co-owners

300 Second Avenue,
Suite 105,
Niwot
652-1606

*T*he influx of high-tech companies moving to Boulder County has brought with it hundreds of people vying for housing. Many have chosen to live in Niwot and, as a result, the demand for new markets and restaurants has surged. Howard Treppeda capitalized on this opportunity by opening an Italian market. In 1996, he convinced Carl Smith to join him.

Treppeda and Smith have been friends since the second grade, growing up together in the Hudson Valley of New York. As adults, they pursued entirely different careers, but managed to keep in touch.

Treppeda was always interested in food and cooking. He has worked in restaurants in Nantucket, the Colorado Rockies and even Boulder, at Lucile's. He also studied at the Culinary Institute of America. After getting married, Treppeda and his bride spent a year working in a restaurant in Amsterdam. "Then we wined and dined our way around Europe, from Czechoslovakia to Italy and Spain." Their stay ended in Beaune, France, where Treppeda cooked at a friend's restaurant. Upon returning to the States, they settled in Colorado.

In the meantime, Smith had become a currency trader on Wall Street and was in no way involved in the food business. He does, however, enjoy fine food and he loves to cook. Opening a specialty market was something he and Treppeda had often dreamed about and discussed. Smith was ready for a change, so it was easy for Treppeda to convince him to move to Niwot.

Treppeda's is reminiscent of neighborhood stores in East Coast cities; you are greeted at the door and the owners know you by name. Treppeda will tell customers, "You've got to try this," or "We just made the best pasta salad." Smith will ask, "Did your husband like the lamb?" or "How's your new car running?"

Not only are Treppeda and Smith nice guys; they're doing a great job. The store is attractive and bright. It is filled with hundreds of offerings, but it is not so cluttered that you can't take everything in. They prepare sandwiches and salads for lunch that can be enjoyed at one of the tables in front of the restaurant, weather permitting. They have delicious, freshly prepared foods to go and Boar's Head and imported meats and cheeses. There are fresh-frozen sauces and stocks, fresh and dried pastas and bread from Daily Bread. There is a wide selection of extra virgin olive oils, along with vinegars and other Italian specialties. Olive and porcini paste to spread on bruschetta are also available. And if you want a quick and easy-to-cook dinner, take home a stuffed flank steak or marinated pork tenderloin to grill. Trepedda shares some special recipes with us here, including a favorite soup from his Italian grandmother.

Italian Spetzal Soup "Pasadine"

Serves: Six to Eight

This recipe was handed down from Howard Treppeda's grandmother. It is truly comfort food, and is a great starter for an Italian dinner. The spetzal can be prepared a day ahead and refrigerated.

2 cups fresh breadcrumbs
2 cups freshly grated Parmesan
      cheese
5 large eggs, lightly beaten
1 tsp. black pepper
⅛ tsp. freshly grated nutmeg*
2 tsp. lemon zest
1 tsp. lemon juice
2 quarts chicken broth (or
      vegetable broth for a
      vegetarian soup)*
salt and pepper
minced fresh parsley to garnish

1. In a large bowl, mix the bread crumbs, Parmesan, eggs, pepper, nutmeg, lemon zest and lemon juice. Mix well and form into two balls. Wrap in plastic wrap and set aside for at least one hour. If not using soon after that, refrigerate until ready to use (within three days).

2. Place the broth in a large saucepan and bring it to a boil. Turn down the heat until the broth is at a slow boil —bubbling, but not a galloping boil. Using the large holes on a cheese grater, grate each of the bread and egg balls into the boiling broth until is reaches the right thickness for your taste (it sounds vague, but try it with a little at a time and see the result). Allow the broth to simmer about 15 minutes. Add salt and pepper to taste. Serve in warm soup bowls and sprinkle with parsley.

TIPS
—Ground nutmeg in a jar is okay, but will have a slightly less intense flavor than freshly ground.
—The Parmesan adds a lot of salty flavor to the soup; be careful not to over-season. If using canned broth, make sure to use a low-sodium brand.

Salmon Fillets with Ginger-Horseradish Roof

Serves: Four

A very simple dish. The "roof" is formed with ginger and horseradish roots. The combination is delicious.

1. Season the salmon with salt and pepper. Combine the gingerroot and horseradish root and mix well. Spread ¼ cup of this mixture on one side of each salmon fillet.

2. Preheat the oven to 425°. Coat the bottom of a large skillet with olive oil. Heat over medium-high heat. When the oil is hot, add the salmon, "roof" side down. Cook for one to two minutes, or until browned. Turn the salmon "roof" side up, place in the oven and bake for three to five minutes, or until done to your taste.

3. While the fish is baking, melt the butter in another skillet. When it is bubbling, add the spinach and toss. Add the water and vinegar and cover the pan. Cook until the spinach is wilted and hot, which should take just a few minutes. Add salt and pepper to taste.

4. Divide the spinach among four warm plates. Top with a salmon fillet, "roof" side up, and garnish with lemon slices. Serve immediately.

4 (6 oz.) salmon fillets
salt and pepper
½ cup peeled, grated
     gingerroot*
½ cup peeled, grated
     horseradish root*
olive oil
2 Tbl. butter
1-1½ lbs. spinach, well cleaned,
     tough stems removed
¼ cup water
1 tsp. cider vinegar
1 lemon, thinly sliced

*TIPS
— It will take one or two of the big knobby gingerroots (not the little ones you break off) to get ½ cup of grated ginger. Look for smooth skin; wrinkled skin indicates aging. Leftover ginger can be preserves by putting it in a jar covered with sherry. It will keep refrigerated for three

months. If you have a food processor, use it to shred the ginger and the horseradish roots.

—Horseradish root is usually available at groceries or produce markets. It looks like a big, round, brownish bulb. Always peel it before using. It is very strong and might make your eyes water. One bulb should be enough to make ½ cup of shredded horseradish.

Chocolate Bread Pudding

Serves: Six to Eight

This delicious dessert may be served with a custard sauce, such as Crème Anglaise (recipe on page 42, but substitute one teaspoon vanilla for the coriander), ice cream or raspberry sauce and whipped cream.

8-10 slices stale white bread, cut into ½" cubes
vegetable oil
2 cups half-and-half (or 1 cup milk and 1 cup heavy cream)
8 oz. good-quality semisweet chocolate*
1 stick butter
½ cup sugar
3 large eggs, slightly beaten
2 tsp. vanilla

1. Preheat the oven to 325°. Place the bread cubes in an oiled 1½ quart baking dish and set aside.

2. Combine the half-and-half, chocolate, butter and sugar in a medium saucepan. Cook over low heat, stirring frequently, until the chocolate has melted. Beat with a wire whisk until the mixture is smooth.

3. Combine the eggs and vanilla. Remove the chocolate mixture from the heat and, whisking constantly, slowly add the egg mixture to the chocolate. Pour the mixture over the bread cubes.

4. Place the baking dish in a water bath (see Before Beginning). Bake for 40 to 45 minutes. Serve warm or cool with desired topping.

*TIPS
—Treppeda suggests using Belgian chocolate. Any chocolate will work, but the better the quality, the better the result.

*N*ineteen miles up beautiful, winding Boulder Canyon from Boulder, is Nederland, home of the Tungsten Grille. The Grille represents the fulfillment of chef-owner Geoff Sherin's longtime dream to open a restaurant in the Boulder area. In August 1995, with the help of his partner, architect and Boulder native, Scott Coburn, his dream came true. Sherin named the restaurant after the abandoned town of Tungsten, located just below Barker Dam, east of Nederland.

How did a young man from Princeton, New Jersey end up in Colorado? Sherin's love of Colorado took root while he was attending Fountain Valley, a prep school near Colorado Springs. After high school, Sherin graduated from Boston University and pursued numerous careers, from show business agent in Los Angeles to fishing guide in Summit County, Colorado. He then discovered cooking and enrolled at the Culinary Institute of America. After graduating, he furthered his education in Italy on a work-study program, an experience which is reflected in many of his dishes.

When Sherin felt he had gained sufficient schooling and experience, he began pursuing his dream. He soon found a location for the Tungsten Grille in the former Mountain Burger restaurant adjacent to the roundabout intersection at the entrance to Nederland.

One of the first things you notice walking through the door of the Grille is the unusual furniture. Sherin commissioned local carpenter, artist and blacksmith Peter Drake and woodworker Dell DelliQuardi to create the unique chairs and tables. Drake also made the countertops and workstations, using wood recycled from the lanes of an old bowling alley.

Sherin describes his food as "rustic Italian and American." The menu contains a variety of comfort foods such as Buffalo wings and barbecue beef ribs alongside risotto of the day and sauteed eggplant sand-

Tungsten Grille

Geoff Sherin, Chef/Owner

Corner of Highways
119 & 72,
Nederland
258-9231

wich. Sherin's goal is "to serve more nutritious, traditional food and at the same time "introduce new cuisine to Nederland." Sherin loves telling the story of a local cowboy and his wife who he talked into trying risotto. "Much to their surprise, they really loved it," he grins.

Sherin confides, "I love sharing my food with this community—this beautiful place . . . I love what I'm doing. I have a great staff and the people (of Nederland) are responding. I'm very lucky!"

Bruschetta Rossa

Serves: Six as an appetizer

1 loaf coarse country-style bread (we used Rudi's Rustics Country French Bread)
½ cup olive oil, plus extra for grilling
4 tomatoes, peeled and chopped into ¼" to ½" pieces (see Before Beginning)
¼ cup finely shredded, lightly packed fresh basil*
1½ tsp. minced garlic
salt and pepper
fresh basil leaves to garnish

1. Slice the bread at an angle to get six ¾" slices. Brush both sides of each slice lightly with olive oil.

2. Combine the olive oil, tomatoes, basil, garlic and olive oil in a bowl. Season with salt and pepper. You can do this a day ahead.

3. Grill or broil the bread on both sides until a light brown crust forms.

4. Using a slotted spoon to drain the tomato mixture, place a generous helping on each slice of bread. Arrange the bruschetta on a platter and garnish with basil leaves.

*TIPS
—To shred basil, roll leaves together into a tight cylinder and slice them, using very fine parallel cuts to produce thin strips.

Roasted Portobello Mushrooms over Field Greens

Serves: Four

An unusual and delicious first course.

2 Tbl. balsamic vinegar
1 Tbl. chopped basil
1 Tbl. chopped thyme
1 Tbl. chopped parsley
Kosher salt and pepper
¼ cup + 2 Tbl. extra virgin
     olive oil
4 portobello mushrooms,*
     stems removed
½ lb. mixed greens
¼ cup grated Parmesan cheese

1. Combine the vinegar, basil, thyme, parsley, salt and pepper. Whisk vigorously for about two minutes. Slowly add the ¼ cup of olive oil in a stream, whisking constantly. This can be made a day ahead.

2. Preheat the oven to 400°. In an oven-proof skillet large enough to hold all four mushrooms (with a little space between them), heat the two tablespoons of oil to the smoking point.* Add the mushrooms and sear on both sides; about three minutes total. Add more oil if needed. Lightly salt and pepper the under-side of the mushrooms, then turn them cap side up. Place the mushrooms in the oven and roast for approximately seven minutes, until tender.

3. While the mushrooms are roasting, toss the greens with just enough of the vinaigrette to coat the leaves. Divide the greens among four plates. Place one mushroom on each portion of greens, drizzle a little vinaigrette over each mushroom and sprinkle with Parmesan. Serve with steak knives.

*TIPS
—If you do not have an oven-proof skillet, transfer the mushrooms to a cookie sheet for baking.
—Our test kitchen tried making this dish with plain white button mushrooms. The results were less than satisfactory compared to using portobellos.

Braised Lamb Shanks on White Bean Ragout

6 lamb shanks, 5 to 6 lbs. total
salt and pepper
flour for dredging
½ cup extra virgin olive oil
7 garlic cloves, crushed
1 large onion, chopped into
    medium-sized pieces
5 stalks celery, chopped into
    medium-sized pieces
2 large carrots, chopped into
    medium-sized pieces
2 cups dry red wine
1 lemon, thinly sliced
1 bay leaf
3 cups beef or veal stock
1 (32 oz.) can crushed Italian
    plum tomatoes
1 tsp. salt
¼ tsp. pepper, or more to taste
White Bean Ragout (recipe
    follows)
fresh rosemary sprigs to
    garnish

Serves: Six

1. Preheat the oven to 325°. Season the lamb shanks with salt and pepper. Dredge in flour to coat.* Heat the olive oil in a large cast iron skillet and brown the shanks on all sides. Remove the shanks from the pan and set aside.

2. Add the garlic, onion, celery and carrots to the same pan. Cover and sweat over low heat for 10 minutes, stirring after five minutes (see Before Beginning). Be careful not to brown the onions.

3. Remove the lid and add one cup of the wine. Raise the heat to high and stir for a few minutes to get all the bits of vegetable and meat off the bottom of the skillet. Add the rest of the wine and remaining ingredients and bring to a low simmer.

4. Return the lamb shanks to the skillet. They should be almost covered by the liquid. Add water if needed. Cover with foil and place in the oven. Bake until the shanks are tender; about three hours. Check after the second hour and add more stock if needed.

5. Remove the shanks from the liquid and keep them warm. Strain the liquid left in the skillet. Return the strained liquid to the pan and heat to boiling. Reduce the liquid to the desired sauce consistency. Serve the shanks on white bean ragout (recipe follows) and moisten with the cooking liquid. Garnish with rosemary sprigs.

*TIPS
—An easy way to coat lamb shanks is to put them in a plastic or paper bag with the flour and shake.

White Bean Ragout

Serves: Six as a side dish

1. Place the beans in a large bowl and cover with water by 5" to 6". Soak the beans overnight. Rinse and drain them before using.

2. In a large saucepan, place the beans, two cloves of the garlic, the bay leaf and one-third of the rosemary. Cover the beans with water and add four cups of the stock. Bring to a boil over high heat, then lower the heat until the beans are just simmering. Cook, uncovered, until the beans are tender; about one hour. Stir occasionally, adding more stock or water as necessary. When the beans are done, cool them in the cooking liquid, then drain and set aside.

3. In a large skillet, heat the olive oil and add the other two cloves of garlic. Cover and cook over low heat for five minutes, being sure not to let it brown. Add the beans and the remaining rosemary. Stir until heated thoroughly. Add the tomatoes, wine and the remaining one cup stock. Cook over high heat until most of the liquid has evaporated. Stir in the Parmesan and butter. Season with salt and pepper. Serve with braised lamb shanks, or as a hearty addition to a vegetarian meal.

2 lbs. dried cannellini beans
    (or other white beans such
    as great Northern)
4 garlic cloves, crushed
1 bay leaf
4 sprigs fresh rosemary,
    minced, or 1 tsp. dried,
    crushed with fingers
5 cups vegetable stock
2 Tbl. extra virgin olive oil
2 cups tomatoes, chopped into
    medium-sized pieces
1 cup dry white wine
¼ cup grated Parmesan
1 Tbl. butter
salt and pepper

White Wave Soy Foods

Steve Demos, Owner

1990 North 57th Court,
Boulder
443-3470

Steve Demos is a product of the late sixties and early seventies. He describes himself and his team at White Wave as "a whole bunch of romantic idealists striving to achieve the hippy Peace Corps days again."

After graduating from college, Demos and a friend (the present CFO of White Wave) hitchhiked from Italy to New Delhi three times over a four-year period. "We lived in caves, beach huts, houseboats and ox carts." The meat was not safe to eat in many of the countries through which they passed – Iran, Turkey, Afghanistan and Pakistan. He remembers, "The last time I ate meat was in the northern hills of Afghanistan. I was ill for three days. When I got back from Asia, I never started eating animal protein again. It was just something I got accustomed to and I stuck with it."

Growing up, Demos' father encouraged him to start his own business, just as he had done. The idea for manufacturing tofu came from Demos' own diet. "I was my own market," he remarks. He realized that no one was supplying any alternative for meat proteins. "Soy had been around for ages but there had been no set of conditions where there had been a willing market and a need and manufacturing base to deliver the product."

While attending a meditation conference in California, Demos began making tofu – experimenting on the conference attendees. He also began developing a business plan. He incorporated into this plan what he calls "right livelihood" – everyone who touches the product benefits from it – a philosophy coming largely from his studies and meditations in India.

Demos chose Boulder as a base because "it's so eclectic...it's people have the highest intent...and it represents some of the most experimental thinking, the most progressive ideas and the most ethical attitudes."

Tofu was the first product White Wave manufac-
tured, but now they distribute over 50 products from
yogurt and cheese to pocket pies and stir-fry meals. "We
are no longer just a tofu company," says Demos. White
Wave's products can be found in over 350 natural food
stores and supermarkets in Colorado and beyond.

Demos says, "Boulder proved to us that (White
Wave) works and then we proved to the natural foods
market nationally that it works."

His philosophy helps explain his success: "You
have to be willing to expend energy and cause friction."

Tempeh Mock Chicken Salad

Serves: Four

1. Cut the tempeh into ½" pieces and steam it for 10
minutes in about ¼-½" of water. Cool.

2. Combine the remaining ingredients and mix well.
Add the tempeh and refrigerate the mixture until ready
to use. Serve just as you would regular chicken salad.

*TIPS
—Tempeh is a firm cake made from fermented soybeans.
It is very high in protein and can be found in health food
stores and most groceries.
—Nutritional yeast is also called Brewer's yeast. It is a
rich source of B vitamins and can be found in health
food stores and in beer-making shops.
—Tamari is made from soybeans. It is similar to regular
soy sauce, but a little thicker. It is available in health
food stores and the Asian food section of many groceries.

8 oz. White Wave Tempeh*
3 Tbl. mayonnaise or soy mayo,
       plus more to your taste
2 Tbl. nutritional yeast*
2 Tbl. chopped dill pickle
2 Tbl. minced parsley
1 tsp. prepared mustard
1 tsp. tamari soy sauce*
1 stalk celery, chopped
¼ medium onion, minced

Boulder Polenta

Serves: Six to Eight

This dish was created especially for White Wave by chef Leonardo Laudisio of Laudisio Ristorante Italiano. It can be prepared up to the baking point a day ahead and baked just before serving.

16 oz. tofu
1 egg
4 oz. Asiago cheese
4 oz. ricotta cheese
⅛ tsp. nutmeg
salt and pepper to taste
1 bunch spinach, cleaned,
    stemmed and chopped
5¼ cups water
salt
6 Tbl. butter (or olive oil)
1 cup polenta*
nutmeg
pepper
grated Parmesan cheese

1. In a large bowl combine the tofu, eggs, cheeses, nutmeg, salt and pepper. Blend well. Add the spinach and mix thoroughly. Spread this mixture in an oiled three-quart baking dish.

2. Bring the water to boil in a medium saucepan. Add a little salt and the butter. When the butter has melted, slowly add the polenta, stirring constantly with a whisk for five minutes. Remove the pan from the heat and stir in a pinch of nutmeg and a little pepper.

3. Pour the polenta mixture over the tofu mixture and place it in the refrigerator for one hour or overnight. Thirty minutes before serving, preheat the oven to 350°. Bake for 20 minutes. Sprinkle with some Parmesan cheese and serve.

*TIPS
—Polenta is a cornmeal product that has become very popular in culinary circles. It can be served soft, grilled, or fried (see Crispy Polenta with Grilled Pears in Gorgonzola Cream, page 80). Polenta is usually available in groceries and Italian markets.

Tofu Enchiladas

Serves: Four to Six

This recipe utilizes soy cheeses as well as tofu. You will be surprised at how tasty these enchiladas are.

1. In a medium saucepan combine the enchilada sauce, tomato sauce, garlic powder, onion, green chilies, chili powder and basil. Bring to a boil then lower the heat and simmer for 15 minutes.

2. Combine the tofu and both Soy-A-Melt cheeses in a bowl for the filling, and mix well.

3. Place soy oil in a medium skillet to a ⅛" depth over medium heat. When the oil is hot, fry the tortillas one at a time until soft. Place some filling in the middle of each tortilla, top it with some sliced olives and roll it up. Place the enchiladas in an oiled 9" x 13" baking dish seam-side down.

4. Preheat the oven to 350°. Cover the enchiladas with the sauce from step 1 and sprinkle with the ¼ cup of Mozzarella Soy-A-Melt. Cover and bake for 15-20 minutes. Serve immediately.

**TIPS*
—Soy-A-Melt is a soy cheese found, along with tofu, in health food stores and many groceries.

14 oz. enchilada sauce
14 oz. tomato sauce
1½ Tbl. garlic powder
1 medium onion, chopped
2 oz. diced green chilies
4 tsp. chili powder
½ tsp. dried basil
16 oz. White Wave tofu, drained and crumbled
6 oz. Soy-A-Melt, cheddar style, grated (or cheddar cheese)*
6 oz. Soy-A-Melt, mozzarella style, grated (or mozzarella cheese)
soy oil
12 corn tortillas
1-2 oz. sliced black olives
¼ cup grated Soy-A-Melt, mozzarella style (or mozzarella cheese)

Fajita Stir Fry

Serves: Two

2-3 Tbl. canola or olive oil
½ red bell pepper, sliced
    ½"-thick
1" piece of ginger root, peeled
    and thinly sliced
1 medium onion, chopped
2 garlic cloves, minced
4 oz. Shitake mushrooms, stems
    removed, sliced ¼" thick
6 oz. White Wave vegetarian
    fajita, cut into strips*
1-2 tsp. toasted sesame oil*
1-2 Tbl. soy sauce
½ cup water
¼ lb. snow peas

1. Heat the oil in a wok or large skillet over high heat. Add the red pepper, ginger and onion. Cook, stirring constantly, until the pepper and onion are soft. Add the garlic and stir fry for one minute. Add the mushrooms and fajita strips and cook for approximately five minutes, until the mushrooms are tender.

2. Stir in the remaining ingredients and bring to a simmer. Cook until the snow peas are crisp-tender. Serve immediately.

*TIPS
—White Wave vegetarian fajita strips are made from a wheat gluten called seitan. It is available in natural food markets and some groceries.
—Toasted sesame oil can be found in Asian markets and the Asian section of grocery stores.

Willow River Cheese Importers

When visiting Willow River Cheese Importers, bring a coat. Once you get inside the 6,000-square-foot refrigerated warehouse and discover all the cheeses and other goodies, you won't want to leave. And after 10 minutes, you will be as well chilled as the groceries. White has, however, thoughtfully included a warm-up area in her French Country Store, adjacent to the warehouse.

The store is a gourmet boutique of sorts where you can find all manner of food items, Italian platters, English teapots, coffees, teas and candies. You can enjoy a cup of tea or espresso while perusing the olive oils and balsamic vinegars, and then have a sandwich or choose from an assortment of prepared foods in the little cafe.

White and her husband started Willow River with only four varieties of cheese. Their goal was to convince folks in the restaurant business to switch from low-quality processed cheeses to the White's natural products made by high-quality cheese makers.

"People weren't into cheese then like they are now," says White. "Most of them didn't even know what Brie was." The Whites visited Boulder County restaurants giving away samples along with recipes to try. Their hard work began to pay off, as many local chefs switched to Willow River cheeses. At the same time, interest in sampling new cheeses increased nationwide. As the demand for different varieties grew, the Whites added new cheeses to their stock and today carry everything from Appenzeller and Deux de Montagne to good old Monterey Jack.

In the beginning, the Whites did business out of an 8x8-foot cooler. They started as a wholesale-only business, but as their cheeses became known, people started asking them to sell retail. "We literally had people knocking on our door asking to buy our cheese." When their lease expired they moved Willow River to its pre-

Linda White, Owner

33 South Pratt Parkway, Longmont
443-4444

sent location and decided to open the retail shop. Their daughter and son now work for Willow River, and their grandson can often be found "in residence" in the offices above the store. "This has always been a labor of love," says White. "Everything just kind of evolved."

Baked Brie with Apricots

Serves: Eight to Ten

Warm Brie covered with apricots and crisp nuts makes a sublime spread for French bread or crackers. Serve this as part of a delectable cheese-and-dessert course.

1 (1 lb.) Brie wheel
6 tsp. Grand Marnier or other orange liqueur
⅓ cup dried apricots, sliced into ¼" strips
3 Tbl. golden raisins
3 Tbl. pine nuts
water biscuits or toasted slices of French bread

1. Preheat the oven to 350°. With a sharp knife, slice off the top rind of the Brie. Place the Brie on an ovenproof serving platter. Using a fork or skewer with thick tines, prick the Brie in a dozen places and drizzle with 1½ tsp. of the Grand Marnier.

2. Toss the apricots, raisins and pine nuts with the remaining 4½ teaspoons of Grand Marnier. Spread this mixture evenly over the top of the Brie. Bake for eight to 10 minutes, or until the cheese softens and is beginning to melt. Serve with water biscuits or toasted bread.

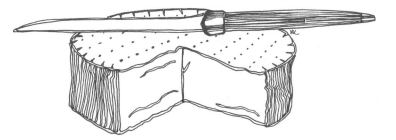

Nine Different Cheese Party Snacks

Serves: As many as you want

These cheese nibbles make easy-to-pass finger food for cocktails or teatime.

Nibble 1. Brush slices of French bread with olive oil and rub the cut side with a garlic clove. Toast or grill the bread, then spread it with goat cheese or top it with a thin slice of mozzarella. Finish with an oil-packed sun-dried tomato. Garnish with basil leaves.

Nibble 2. On wooden skewers, alternate cubes of Jarlsberg, cheddar or Jack cheese with strawberries, melon balls and fresh pineapple.

Nibble 3. On wooden skewers, alternate cubes of Jack or white Cheddar cheese with seedless red and green grapes.

Nibble 4. On wooden skewers, alternate cubes of dry Monterey Jack cheese with cubes of papaya.

Nibble 5. Stuff cherry tomato halves with fresh, herb-flavored mild white goat cheese or natural cream cheese. Garnish with a basil leaf.

Nibble 6. Dollop Saint André cheese (a mild, triple-cream cheese available at specialty stores) on dried apricots and sprinkle with chopped, toasted pistachios or chopped, peeled and toasted hazelnuts.

Nibble 7. Halve figs and spread them with mascarpone cheese and top them with a strip of prosciutto.

Nibble 8. Halve figs, top them with Gorgonzola cheese and broil until heated through.

Nibble 9. Spread toasted slices of French bread with fresh, mild white goat cheese and top with red pepper pesto, black olive spread (olivetti) or a few dried cherries.

Spinach Salad with Strawberries and Feta Cheese

12 oz. spinach, rinsed well, tough stems removed
1 cup strawberry halves
4 oz. feta cheese, crumbled
¼ cup pistachios, shelled and toasted
Raspberry Vinaigrette (recipe follows)

Serves: Six

Place the spinach, strawberries, feta and pistachios in a large bowl. Use enough dressing to just moisten the spinach and toss. Add more dressing if needed, but do not overdress. Serve immediately on chilled salad plates.

Pear, Gorgonzola and Walnut Salad

2 heads of endive
3 Comice pears, peeled and sliced
6 oz. Gorgonzola cheese, crumbled
½ cup walnuts, toasted
Raspberry Vinaigrette (recipe follows)

Serves: Six

Arrange the endive leaves in a fan shape on chilled salad plates. Top with pear slices and sprinkle with Gorgonzola and walnuts. Drizzle with a little of the dressing.

Papaya, Goat Cheese and Pistachio Salad

1 head Bibb lettuce, rinsed, dried, and torn into large pieces
4 oz. arugula, rinsed and dried
2 ripe papayas, peeled, seeded and sliced
6 oz. mild white goat cheese
¼ cup pistachios, shelled and toasted
Raspberry Vinaigrette (recipe follows)

Serves: Six

Mix all of the ingredients with enough dressing to just moisten the lettuce. Serve on chilled salad plates.

Spinach Salad with Tangerines and Pine Nuts

Serves: Six

In a large bowl, toss the spinach with enough dressing to just moisten it. Divide the spinach among chilled salad plates. Top the spinach with tangerine sections, avocado chunks, a few shavings of Parmesan and a sprinkling of pine nuts. Drizzle a little more of the dressing over each salad and serve.

12   oz. spinach, rinsed well, tough stems removed
2 tangerines, peeled and sectioned
2 avocados, peeled, seeded and cut into large chunks
4 oz. Parmesan cheese, shaved with a cheese shaver or sharp knife
¼ cup pine nuts, toasted
Raspberry Vinaigrette (recipe follows)

Raspberry Vinaigrette

Makes: Enough to dress a salad serving Six

This dressing goes well with all of the preceding Cheese and Nut Salads.

Whisk the vinegar, lemon juice and Dijon mustard in a small bowl, until the mustard is incorporated into the liquid. Add the garlic, salt, pepper and oils, whisking constantly.

3 Tbl. raspberry vinegar
3 Tbl. fresh lemon juice
1 tsp. Dijon mustard
1 garlic clove, minced
½ tsp. salt
¼ tsp. pepper
¾ cup light olive oil
½ cup canola oil

Zolo Grill

Joe Schneider,
Head Chef

2525 Arapahoe Avenue,
Boulder
449-0444

*J*oe Shneider describes his food as having a California base fused with Carribean and Southwestern flavors. Working with this complex mix, he pays particular attention to the intricacies of the flavors, being careful not to overwhelm the inherent qualities of the individual ingredients in a dish.

Schneider grew up in Santa Barbara, the son of a mechanical engineer. "My father owns a shop where he works on Porsches and BMWs. All my life I figured that I would eventually take over the business. That's what the oldest son always does," says Schneider. That was not, however, the direction he ultimately followed.

"I always loved cooking for my family," Schneider says. "There are seven of us, so it was always quite a production." At the age of 15, he started working part-time as a dishwasher in a local restaurant. Since then, he has not gone longer than a few months without a job in a restaurant.

In 1989, Schneider enrolled at the California Culinary Institute in San Francisco. While there, he externed at the famed champagnery Domain Chandon in the Napa Valley. After graduation he returned to Napa, working at the Silverado Country Club and for the Christian Brothers' restaurant. "I honed my bread-making, among other skills that I didn't have time to perfect in school."

After two and a half years, Schneider headed home to Santa Barbara. It was there that he was able to work for a restaurateur and chef who allowed him the freedom to try out new ideas and taste combinations. "That was the first time I ever felt so challenged. I would go to the book store everyday and spend two or three hours before work planning what I was going to do that night." It was during this time that Schneider began trying Caribbean dishes.

To learn more about this unusual cuisine he moved to Florida. Working at Louie's Back Yard in Key West, he experimented with different Caribbean seasonings and ingredients, "fresh fruit—exotic stuff like carambolas, mangoes, sapotes and huge Asian papayas." He worked with many varieties of chiles and composed dozens of different salsas. He soon realized that Caribbean cuisine is very similar to Southwestern cuisine and he began combining flavors from both in his cooking.

Schneider left Florida in 1995. He missed the West and he wanted to be closer to home. He arrived in Boulder in July 1995. "I didn't know a soul," he says. "I bought a phone book, visited the Chamber of Commerce and just started talking to people." He ended up taking a job at Zolo Grill, and ultimately took over the kitchen.

And what does Schneider think of his decision to move to here? "I love Boulder—the size of the town, the mix of people—it's so diverse, from the students to the die-hard athletes. It's great to be exposed to so much."

Smoked Shrimp and Fennel Tamales with Goat Cheese

Makes: Ten tamales

Be sure to allow at least an hour for the corn husks to soak, plus time to make the yam broth for the masa.

1 lb. smoked shrimp, peeled and coarsely chopped*
1 bulb fennel, trimmed, chopped and steamed until tender (use the white part only)
2 pablano chilies, stems, seeds and membranes removed, and cut into thin strips
1 large red bell pepper, seeds and membranes removed, and cut into thin strips
1 bunch green onions, root ends trimmed and cut into thin strips at an angle
2 cups Haystack Mountain goat cheese*
salt and pepper
chile molido*
ground cumin
2 sticks butter, softened
2½ cups masa*
(ingredients continued on page 185)

1. Combine the shrimp, fennel, pablano chiles, bell pepper, green onions and goat cheese in a bowl and mix well. Season to taste with salt, pepper, chile molido and cumin. Set aside.

2. Place the butter in a mixing bowl and beat until fluffy using the paddle attachment. Add the masa and beat until it is incorporated thoroughly into the butter. Add the yam broth (recipe follows) and beat.* Add the honey and season to taste with salt, pepper, chile molido and cumin.

3. Drain the corn husks and lay each one flat. Place approximately ¾ cup of the masa mixture into the middle of each husk, spreading it slightly. Place ¼ cup of the filling in the center of the masa. Using the husk, roll the sides of the masa up over the filling. Wrap the husk completely around the masa and filling, and twist the tapered end of the husk to keep it in place.

4. Put the rolled husks in a steamer or on a plate over boiling water (see "steaming" in Before Beginning). Cover and steam for 12 minutes.

5. To serve, ladle a generous amount of mole rojo onto a warmed plate and place one or more of the steamed

husks on top. Peel back the top seam of the husk, exposing the tamale. Squirt some roasted corn crema on top and serve immediately. Garnish with sprigs of cilantro.

For the yam broth, heat the olive oil in a medium saucepan over medium-low heat. When the oil is hot add the onion and cook until it is almost soft. Add the garlic and cook a little longer. Add the water and yam, and cook until the yam is soft. Add the cilantro. Transfer mixture to a blender and puree. Strain and cool to room temperature.

*TIPS

—If smoked shrimp are unavailable, substitute grilled shrimp. Toss a handful of wood chips that have been soaked in water on the coals and close the lid. Be careful not to overcook (medium shrimp take about five minutes). The best flavor results if the shrimp are cooked with the shells intact. Remove the shells after cooking.

—Haystack Mountain Goat Cheese is a Boulder County-made cheese available at many groceries along the Front Range of Colorado. If you cannot find it, substitute any good goat cheese.

—Chile molido is a type of chile powder. Substitute cayenne pepper if it is unavailable.

—Masa is a Mexican cornmeal, also called harina. It is the corn flour used to make corn tortillas. It is available in most groceries or Latin markets.

—Packaged, dried corn husks are available in most groceries or Latin markets.

2½ cups yam broth (recipe follows)
2 Tbl. honey
10 corn husks soaked in water for at least 1 hour*
fresh cilantro sprigs to garnish (optional)
mole rojo(recipe follows on p. 186)
roasted corn crema (recipe follows on p. 187)
1 Tbl. olive oil
1 small onion, chopped
2 cloves garlic, chopped
1¾ cups water
1 medium yam, peeled and cut into 1" pieces
1 Tbl. chopped fresh cilantro
cilantro to garnish

Mole Rojo

2 Tbl. olive oil

1½ medium yellow onions, chopped

3 tomatillos, skins removed, charred under the broiler or on a gas stove, and chopped

5 Roma tomatoes, charred and chopped

3 pasilla chiles, stems and seeds removed, lightly toasted*

3 ancho chiles, stems and seeds removed, lightly toasted*

2 mulato chiles, stems and seeds removed, lightly toasted*

4 cups water

2 ripe bananas, coarsely chopped

¼ cup sun-dried cherries

2½ Tbl. sesame seeds, toasted

¼ cup almond slices, toasted

2 red chile corn tortillas, toasted (or ½ cup crushed red chile corn tortilla chips)*

2 cloves roasted garlic, peeled after roasting, and chopped

1 tsp. cinnamon

pinch ground cloves

¼ tsp. pepper

¼ tsp. allspice

½ tsp. salt

1½ oz. Ibarra chocolate*

1 oz. unsweetened chocolate

Makes: approximately Four cups

The chiles called for in this recipe are dried. This sauce is also good with grilled chicken or pork.

1. Heat olive oil over medium heat in a large saucepan. Add the onions and cook until they are beginning to brown. Add the tomatillos and tomatoes and cook for two to three minutes. Add the remaining ingredients except for the two chocolates.

2. Simmer the mixture for 30 minutes. Add both chocolates and remove from the heat. Stir until melted. Let the mixture rest for 20 minutes, then purée it in the blender and strain. The sauce is ready to use.

*TIPS

—Pasilla chiles are called Chilacas when they are fresh. Pasillas are also called chile negro. They are medium-hot and found at many grocery stores and Latin markets.

—Ancho chiles are called poblanos when they are fresh. They are the most commonly used dried chile in Mexico, and along with pasilla chiles and mulato chiles, a must for a true mole sauce. They come in three grades with "primero" being the best. They are fairly mild chiles.

—Mulato chiles are in all mole preparations. They have a slightly smoky flavor. They can be found at Latin markets and some groceries. Mulato chiles are graded the same as ancho chiles. They are mild to medium in heat.

—If you use chips, cut down on the amount of salt you add. The chips usually come salted.

—Ibarra chocolate is a specialty item that can be found in Latin and other specialty markets.

Roasted Corn Crema

Makes: approximately Two cups

This sauce is good for garnishing and adding extra flavor to the Smoked Shrimp Tamales and the two chicken recipes that follow.

1. Place the corn kernels in a large skillet, preferably cast iron. Do not add any oil to the pan. Over medium-high heat, roast the corn, stirring often, until it is starting to brown. Cool and set aside.

2. Heat the olive oil over medium heat in a medium saucepan. Add the onion, cover and cook, stirring often, until the onions are soft. Remove the lid and lower the heat. Cook the onions until they have caramelized and are a rich brown color. Cool.

3. Mix the corn and onions with the remaining ingredients. Purée the mixture in batches in a blender. Strain. The crema is now ready to use.

4 cups kernels removed from
    ears of fresh corn
2 Tbl. olive oil
1 small onion, chopped
2 Tbl. roasted garlic (see Before
    Beginning)
1 cup plain yogurt
½ cup sour cream
½ cup vegetable broth or water
1 tsp. fresh thyme leaves,
    chopped
1 tsp. cumin

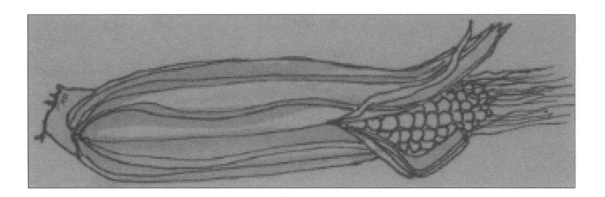

Achiote Chicken Breasts

Serves: Four

Schneider serves this delicious chicken sliced over Pine Nut-Asiago Risotto (recipe follows on p. 189). It is very easy to prepare, but you must allow 24 hours for the chicken to marinate, so plan ahead.

¼ cup achiote paste*
juice of 4 oranges
juice of 4 limes
3 cloves garlic, chopped
2 Tbl. chopped cilantro
½ tsp. ground cumin
¼ tsp. pepper
pinch of salt
4 large chicken breast halves*

1. Place all ingredients except chicken into a blender and puree. Do not strain. Pour the marinade over the chicken and mix to coat well. Place the chicken in the refrigerator for 24 hours. Stir the chicken two or three times during this period.

2. Bring the chicken to room temperature before cooking. Remove the chicken from the marinade, saving some marinade for basting. Grill the chicken over medium-high coals until it is done to your liking. Baste the chicken with some of the marinade while it is cooking. Slice the chicken against the grain and place it on helpings of risotto.

*TIPS
—Achiote paste is the ground seeds of the annatto tree. It is from the Yucatan peninsula and can be found in Latin, Spanish and specialty markets.
—Schneider uses large chicken breast halves with the tenderloin attached. They can be bone-in or boneless, with skin or skinless. Each breast of a chicken is make up of two parts. The small half, called a tenderloin or fillet, contains a white tendon which should be removed.

Pine Nut-Asiago Risotto

Serves: Four

1. Heat the olive oil over medium heat in a medium skillet. Add the onion and cook until it is soft. Add the rice and stir until it becomes slightly translucent.

2. Add the chicken stock ½ cup at a time, stirring after each addition until the liquid is absorbed. When approximately ½ cup of the stock is left, add it along with the cream, cheese and nuts and raise the heat. When the liquid has absorbed, the rice should be "al dente" and bound with a creamy sauce. Serve immediately.

1 Tbl. olive oil
1 medium yellow onion, chopped
½ lb. arborio rice (see "risotto" in Before Beginning)
1 qt. chicken (or vegetable) stock, cold
2 Tbl. heavy cream
¼ cup grated Asiago cheese
½ cup pine nuts, toasted

Mango-Pineapple Salsa

Makes: approximately Two cups

Combine all of the ingredients except the salt and chile molido. Season to taste with salt and chile molido. Store covered in the refrigerator until ready to use.

*TIPS
—Scotch bonnet chiles are among the hottest, be very careful handling them. See Before Beginning.

1 ripe pineapple, trimmed and chopped
2 ripe mangoes, peeled, seeded and chopped
1 scotch bonnet or 1 habanero chile, seeded and minced*
1 poblano chile, seeded and minced
1 red bell pepper, seeded and finely chopped
2 Tbl. chopped fresh mint
juice of one orange
juice of 2 limes
salt
chile molido (see Tips, page 185)

Jerk Chicken

Serves: Four

2 cups fresh squeezed orange
    juice
6 Tbl. chopped cilantro
6 Tbl. fresh thyme leaves
6 Tbl. chopped Italian parsley
6 Tbl. chopped fresh oregano
12 green onions, chopped
3 Tbl. salt
2 Tbl. pepper
1 large mango, peeled, seeded
    and coarsely chopped*
1 fresh habanero pepper, seeded
    and chopped*
½ cup spicy Creole-style
    mustard*
¼ cup sherry vinegar
1 whole fryer chicken (2½-3 lbs.)

The chicken needs to marinate for 24 hours. Serve with Mango-Pineapple Salsa (recipe follows).

1. Place all of the ingredients except the chicken in a blender and puree. Do not strain. Pour the marinade over the chicken and refrigerate it for at least 24 hours. Turn the chicken several times during this period.

2. Remove the chicken from the marinade and bake, broil or grill until done to your liking, basting often with the marinade. Cut the chicken into pieces and serve with mango-pineapple salsa.

*TIPS
—For mangoes see Tips, page 49.
—Habanero chiles are among the hottest, be very careful handling them. See "chiles" in Before Beginning.
—Creole-style mustard can be found in specialty stores.

INDEX

INDEX

INDEX

INDEX

INDEX

INDEX

INDEX

Notes

Notes

About the Author

Janis Judd has lived in Boulder for 20 years. She is a registered nurse and has a degree in business, but her true passion has always been food. She has studied cooking in Paris and with Giuliano Bugialli, Julia Child, Richard Grausman, Bruce Healy and Lynne Rossetto Kasper. She has assisted chefs at the Cooking School of the Rockies and has written two cookbooks for family and close friends: *Help for the Helpless* (for college students) and *Comfort Food*. Two cookbooks benefitting the Colorado Music Festival were compiled by Judd and she published a cooking newsletter in 1994 and 1995 called *Bill of Fare*. She has catered many dinners and parties, but the dream-come-true for Judd was being "chef for a day" at the Pearl Street Inn under Bradford Heap (now chef-owner of the Full Moon Grill). Judd lives in north Boulder with her husband Dick. They have a combined family of five grown children.

Janis Judd's Prize Winning Apple Pie

Serves: 8

This pie won the silver medal at the 1997 National Pie Championships in the Amateur Division, Traditional Apple Pie. The author admits that this is not health food. She uses the lard and vinegar pastry recipe of old for the tender, flaky crust (Don't worry, there is no vinegar taste in the finished product). Two kinds and textures of apples are used to make the pie more interesting.

For the pastry:

1. Place the flour and salt in a food processor. Add the butter and lard and pulse a few times until the fat is in approximately. ¼" pieces (this can be done by hand).

2. Mix the vinegar and 2 Tbl. of the water, and add it to the flour mixture. Pulse two or three times to distribute the liquid. Add another 2 Tbl. of water and pulse several times until the water is well distributed. The mixture should hold together when pressed with your fingers. Add more ice water by teaspoons if the dough is too dry.

3. Dump the mixture onto a work surface and gather it together into a ball. Using the heel of your hand, quickly smear the dough across the work surface several times. This will blend the butter and lard. Do not over work the dough or it will become tough. Form the dough into a round, flat disk and wrap in plastic. Refrigerate the dough for at least one hour.

4. Let the dough sit out for a few minutes to warm it up before working with it. Roll out half the dough for the bottom crust and place it in a 9" deep dish pie plate. Fill the crust as described below, then roll out the other half of the dough for the top crust. Complete as directed below.

2 cups flour
½ tsp. salt
1 stick unsalted butter, chilled and cut into 8 pieces
3 Tbl. cold lard, cut into small pieces
1 Tbl. distilled white vinegar
4-5 Tbl. ice water

3 Granny Smith apples (apx. 1 lb.),
    peeled, cored and chopped
1 Tbl. fresh lemon juice
1 stick + 2 Tbl. unsalted butter
large pinch salt
⅓ cup golden brown sugar
¼ tsp. freshly grated nutmeg
2 Tbl. dark rum
½ tsp. vanilla

For filling 1, combine all of the ingredients except the rum and vanilla in a medium saucepan. Cover and cook over medium-low heat for 30 to 40 minutes, stirring occasionally. When the fruit is very soft and a golden brown color, add the rum and vanilla. Cook for five more minutes. Remove from the heat and mash the apples as you would for mashed potatoes. Season to taste with lemon juice, sugar, nutmeg or rum. Set aside.

5 Yellow Delicious apples, peeled,
    cored and thinly sliced
2 Tbl. fresh lemon juice
½ cup golden brown sugar
2 Tbl. flour (and more if needed)
1½ tsp. cinnamon
zest of 1 lemon
1½ tsp. vanilla
¼ tsp. freshly grated nutmeg
4 Tbl. butter cut into small pieces

For filling 2, toss the apples with lemon juice and sugar. Allow the mixture to sit for a few minutes until the apples release their liquid. Add the flour and combine well (add more flour if the mixture is too soupy). Add the cinnamon, lemon zest, vanilla and nutmeg and blend well.

To assemble the pie:
1. Preheat the oven to 350°. Spread half the apple slices (filling 2) in the bottom crust. Top with all of the mashed apples (filling 1). Evenly place the remaining apple slices atop the mashed apples. Dot the apples with the butter.

2. Roll out the top pastry. Cut vents in the dough (or small hearts or other shapes, reserving the shapes to place on the pie before baking). Place the crust over the apples and trim the edges. Press the edges together to seal and form your favorite decorative edges. If using cut out shapes, place them decoratively around the pie or inside the cut out shapes in the dough. Sprinkle the top with granulated sugar and place in the oven. Bake for 45 to 60 minutes to an hour, until the crust is brown and the apples slices are tender. Allow the pie to cool for 15 minutes or more before serving. The pie is great served warm with slices of cheddar cheese or vanilla ice cream.

To order more copies of

Boulder Cooks

Please send me _____copies of **Boulder Cooks** at a cost of $18.95 plus $3.25 each shipping. Enclosed is a check for $_____. Please make check payable to 3D PRESS.

Name_____

Mailing Address_____

_____**Zip**_____

This is a gift! Please send to:

Name_____

Mailing Address_____

_____**Zip**_____

• •

Name_____

Mailing Address_____

_____**Zip**_____

This is a gift! Please send to:

Name_____

Mailing Address_____

_____**Zip**_____

Send to: 3D Press, PO Box 7402, Boulder, Colorado 80306-7402
To charge with American Express, Master Card or Visa, please call 1 800 408 1376.
Also available from 3D PRESS, *Asheville Cooks* and *Telluride Cooks*, and Bill St. John's *Colorado Restaurants.*